MW00884713

LIFE SKILLS PLAYBOOK
FOR TEEN GIRLS

*Essential Tips for Independence, Confidence, and Success So
You Can Thrive at Life*

ALEX AND RILEY HARPER

LIFE SKILLS PLAYBOOK
FOR TEEN GIRLS

TABLE OF CONTENTS

INTRODUCTION

Hey there, fabulous teen! Welcome to your ultimate guide on a journey that'll not only empower you but also make you burst out laughing (because who says learning can't be fun?). Imagine yourself, standing tall and confident, ready to face anything that comes your way. This book is designed especially for you, teenage girls, to master the art of life with all its twists and turns.

So, why are we talking about life skills? What's the big deal? Well, imagine stepping out of your comfort zone at the end of high school, feeling like an absolute boss because you already know how to cook a mean spaghetti, keep track of your finances without breaking a sweat, and manage your time like a seasoned pro. Doesn't that sound awesome? Mastering life skills will set you up for so much success that you'll practically be walking on air, ready to tackle any challenges life throws at you.

Think of these life skills as your secret superpowers. Knowing how to budget your money means you won't have to live off instant noodles forever (unless you really like them, in which case, no judgment). Understanding how to manage your time means less stress during finals week and more time for binge-watching your favorite shows. And let's not even start on the confidence boost you'll get from knowing you can handle whatever comes your way.

Different chapters in this book cover different life skills, each one vital for your journey toward independence. We're going to dive into everything from cooking basics (so you don't have to Google "how to boil an egg" ever again), to personal finance (because math doesn't have to be boring), to effective communication (because knowing how to speak your mind is crucial for world domination—or, you know, just daily life).

Now, before you freak out and think, "Ugh, another textbook!" let me assure you, this book is anything but. It's written in a language that's totally relatable, like your BFFs texting you advice. We're going to laugh, we might cry (happy tears!), and most importantly, we're going to grow together. By the time you finish this book, you'll be a life-skills ninja with the prowess to impress anyone and everyone around you.

Navigating through this book is going to be a breeze. Think of it as a fun road trip where every chapter is a pit stop brimming with exciting new knowledge and activities. Don't just read—engage with the content! Jot down notes, doodle in the margins, and most importantly, try out the exercises and tips we provide. The more you practice, the easier these skills will become second nature. Each skill you gain is a building block to foundation-shaking awesomeness!

And hey, once you've read a chapter, take a moment to reflect. Ask yourself, "Which of these skills do I need to work on?" or "How can I incorporate this into my everyday life?" Don't just rush through; pause and think about how these nuggets of wisdom apply to you personally. Reflection is a key part of growth. It's like watering a plant; without it, you won't see those beautiful blossoms of confidence and competence.

In every chapter, you'll find little prompts and challenges designed to put what you've learned into practice right away. Don't skip these! They are crafted to help solidify your skills and give you real-world applications. For instance, after reading about budgeting, try creating a spending plan for the next month and see how well you stick to it. After diving into time management, map out your weekly schedule and discover where you can squeeze in some "me-time". Trust me, these small steps will lead to giant leaps in your personal development.

And here's the best part—this book is not just about serious stuff. We're going to have some laughs along the way. Real-life examples, funny anecdotes, and quirky tips will make you chuckle while you learn. Life is too short to be serious all the time, and mastering life skills doesn't mean losing your sense of humor. Quite the contrary—it means you'll have more headspace to actually enjoy life's lighter moments.

So, grab a comfy seat, maybe your favorite snack, and dive in. You're about to embark on a transformative journey that's equal parts enlightening and entertaining. This is your space to grow, to laugh, to challenge yourself, and to come out stronger on the other side. By the end of this ride, you're not just going to feel ready for adulthood—you're going to rock it.

Happy reading and here's to becoming the best version of YOU!

CHAPTER 1

BUILDING CONFIDENCE AND SELF-ESTEEM

Strategies for Understanding Self-Worth and Fostering a Positive Body Image

Are you ready to embrace your self-worth and cultivate a healthy body image? Every teenage girl deserves to master these essential skills. The challenges of evolving bodies, societal expectations, and the constant barrage of seemingly perfect social media influencers can feel like navigating a stormy sea. This chapter serves as your compass, guiding you through these turbulent times and empowering you to emerge with confidence and self-assurance.

Inside, we'll explore ways to recognize and celebrate your unique qualities, because guess what? You are awesome just the way you are. We'll kick things off by making a personal list of strengths and achievements that will serve as your confidence booster. Then, you'll learn how to seek feedback from friends and family to see yourself in a new light. We'll dive into the benefits of keeping a journal, where you can document your wins and track your growth over time.

Celebrating achievements—big or small—will become your new favorite habit. By the end of this chapter, you'll have all the tools you need to build a more positive self-image and resilience against those pesky negative influences.

Identifying Personal Strengths and Achievements

Alright, so let's get into it! Understanding and celebrating our unique qualities can be such a game-changer for self-esteem. It all starts with recognizing what makes us special. One cool way to do this is by creating a personal list of strengths and achievements. Seriously, grab a notebook or open up a notes app on your phone, and start jotting down everything you're proud of. Whether it's being an excellent friend, acing a test, making someone laugh, or even baking a killer batch of cookies—write it all down. No accomplishment is too big or too small.

Now, don't just stop at writing these down. Think about what skills or characteristics helped you achieve these things. Are you a good listener? Maybe you're super organized or have a knack for staying calm in stressful situations. The more specifics you can add to your list, the better you'll understand your own unique brand of awesomeness. Plus, having this list handy is great for those days when you're feeling a little meh and need a quick confidence boost.

What about getting some input from the people who know you best? Sometimes we're our own worst critics and don't see our strengths as clearly as others do. Try asking your friends and family what they think your best qualities are. You might be surprised by what they say! Send out a text or make it a fun conversation over dinner. Not only will you feel good hearing their positive feedback, but it can also help you see yourself from a different perspective.

Okay, onto journaling. Keeping a journal might sound cliché, but it's actually really powerful. Use it to document your successes and the compliments you receive. Let's say you finished a big project or a stranger complimented your style—write it down! When you're feeling down, flipping through your journal can remind you of all the amazing things you've done and the nice things people have said about you. It's like a personalized pep talk right there in your hands.

Another awesome thing about journaling is that it helps you track your growth over time. A year from now, you can look back and see how much you've accomplished and how far you've come. Plus, it doesn't have to be just words. Feel free to add photos, doodles, or anything else that celebrates your wins.

Lastly, and super importantly, let's talk about celebrating achievements. We often wait for the big milestones to celebrate, but why not cheer for the smaller victories too? Did you finally finish that book you've been reading forever? Celebrate it! Managed to get out of bed and face a tough day? Celebrate it! Life is made up of these little moments, and recognizing them can make a huge difference in building self-esteem.

Take a moment each day or week to pat yourself on the back. How you choose to celebrate is up to you. It could be treating yourself to your favorite snack, spending time doing something you love, or even just taking a few minutes to reflect on what you've achieved. The key is to acknowledge and appreciate your efforts regularly.

Remember, building self-esteem doesn't happen overnight. It's about forming habits that help you recognize and appreciate your unique qualities and accomplishments. By making your list of strengths, seeking feedback from loved ones, keeping a journal, and celebrating all your wins—big and small—you're setting yourself up for a more positive self-image and greater resilience against negative influences.

Techniques to Overcome Negative Self-Talk

Let's focus on something super important—recognizing and challenging those sneaky negative thoughts. Building a positive mindset can genuinely transform how you see yourself and everything around you. Are you up for the challenge?

First things first, let's talk about spotting negative self-talk. You know that little voice in your head that sometimes says, "I can't do this," or "I'm not good enough?" Yeah, that's negative self-talk. The trick is to catch it when it happens. One way to do this is to keep a journal where you jot down these thoughts whenever they pop up. Over time, you'll start to see patterns. Maybe you notice that you tend to be harsh on yourself after a tough day at school, or when you're scrolling through social media. Recognizing these triggers can help you become more aware of when negative self-talk occurs.

Now that we've got a handle on identifying negative thoughts, let's move on to reframing them into something positive. This might sound a bit cheesy, but trust me, it works. Instead of thinking, "I'm terrible at math," try flipping it to, "Math is challenging for me, but I'm working hard to get better." It's like taking a bad situation and giving it a positive twist. Think of it as changing the filter on your camera from black and white to bright and colorful. To make this easier, you can create a list of go-to positive affirmations. Keep it handy, maybe even on a sticky note on your mirror, so you see it every day.

Another cool technique is questioning the validity of those nasty negative thoughts. Sometimes our brain likes to play tricks on us, making mountains out of molehills. When a negative thought pops up, ask yourself, "Is this really true?" For example, if you think, "Nobody likes me," take a moment to consider the evidence. Is it really nobody, or is it just one person who was grumpy today? More often than not, you'll find that your negative thoughts are based on assumptions rather than facts.

One last tip—and this one's super fun—is to make visual boards filled with positive mantras and goals. You can call it your "Positivity Board" and fill it with quotes that make you feel good, pictures of things that inspire you, and goals you want to achieve. Every time you look at your board, it'll be a reminder of all the awesome things you're aiming for and all the positivity you're bringing into your life. You could even have a crafting party with friends to make it more enjoyable!

Setting and Maintaining Personal Boundaries

Let's envision this scenario: you've just finished a grueling day at school, and your phone buzzes with yet another invitation to hang out, even though all you want is some quality "me time." It's moments like these when understanding personal boundaries can be a real lifesaver.

Understanding Boundaries:

So, what are personal boundaries? Think of them as invisible lines that protect your physical and emotional space. They define what's okay and what's not okay for you. For example, maybe you're cool with sharing notes but not your secrets. Or perhaps you don't mind lending your clothes, but your phone is off-limits. Boundaries keep you feeling safe and respected. Without them, you might end up feeling overwhelmed or taken advantage of. They're like the rules of your personal bubble and, trust me, everyone needs a bubble.

Why do these boundaries matter? Well, they help you maintain healthy relationships. When you know your limits, you can communicate them clearly to others. This way, people understand how to treat you, and you avoid unnecessary stress and conflict. Plus, having boundaries boosts your self-respect because you're standing up for what you need and deserve.

Identifying Personal Limits:

Now, let's talk about figuring out where your boundaries lie. This can be a bit tricky, especially when you're still discovering who you are. Start by paying attention to your feelings in different situations. Do you feel comfortable or uneasy? Happy or stressed? Excited or drained? Your emotions are great indicators of your limits.

For instance, let's say you're at a party, and someone starts asking really personal questions. If you start feeling anxious or annoyed, that's a huge flashing sign that this conversation is crossing your boundary. It's important to listen to these signals. Ignoring them might lead to bigger issues, like feeling resentful or burned out.

Here's a little exercise: think back to recent experiences where you felt either super comfortable or really uncomfortable. Jot down what was happening in each scenario. Were there common factors? Maybe you felt relaxed when hanging out with friends who respect your need for quiet time but tense when around those who push you to be louder. By reflecting on these moments, you'll get a clearer picture of your personal boundaries.

Communicating Boundaries:

Okay, now that you've identified your boundaries, how do you tell others without sounding like a drama queen? You can do this assertively yet respectfully. Assertiveness means expressing yourself confidently without being aggressive.

First, use "I" statements. Instead of saying, "You always invade my privacy!" rephrase it to, "I feel uncomfortable when my personal space isn't respected." This shifts the focus from blaming to explaining how something affects you. People are more likely to respond positively when they don't feel attacked.

Second, keep it simple and direct. There's no need for long-winded explanations. A straightforward, "Hey, I'm not comfortable with hugging," gets the point across clearly. If a friend keeps borrowing your stuff without asking, gently say, "Could you please ask before taking my things?"

Third, practice makes perfect! Role-play with a trusted friend or in front of a mirror. It might feel awkward at first, but the more you rehearse, the easier it becomes. And remember, it's totally fine to reinforce your boundaries if people forget or cross them again. Just remind them politely, "Remember when we talked about asking before borrowing? I'd appreciate it if you could do that."

Reassessing Boundaries:

Here's a fun fact: boundaries aren't set in stone. They can change over time, and that's perfectly normal. As you grow and experience new things, your comfort levels will shift. What was once a big deal might become a non-issue, and vice versa.

Make it a habit to regularly check in with yourself. Ask, "Are my current boundaries still serving me well?" For example, maybe you once needed lots of alone time after school to recharge, but now you find that hanging out with friends lifts your spirits. It's okay to adjust your boundaries to match your current needs.

Sometimes, external changes might call for boundary tweaks too. Starting a part-time job, joining a new club, or even altering your study schedule can impact how you manage your time and energy. Don't hesitate to reevaluate and reset your boundaries accordingly. Flexibility here is key to maintaining balance and avoiding burnout.

Another tip is to seek feedback from trusted friends and family. They can offer insights on whether your boundaries seem too rigid or too loose. Just make sure these are people who genuinely care about your well-being and respect your space. They can provide a fresh perspective that might highlight areas you hadn't considered.

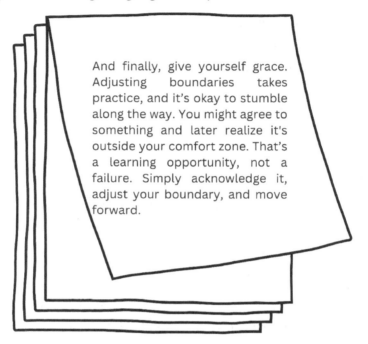

And finally, give yourself grace. Adjusting boundaries takes practice, and it's okay to stumble along the way. You might agree to something and later realize it's outside your comfort zone. That's a learning opportunity, not a failure. Simply acknowledge it, adjust your boundary, and move forward.

Wrapping Up

In this chapter, we've talked about how awesome it can be to recognize your strengths and achievements. Making a list of what makes you unique, asking friends and family for their thoughts, and keeping a journal are great ways to boost your self-esteem. Celebrating even the little wins helps too. These small but powerful habits help you see just how amazing you really are, giving you a solid foundation to stand strong against any negative vibes that come your way.

As we wrap up, remember that building confidence isn't something that happens overnight. It's a journey that involves consistently appreciating your unique qualities and milestones. By focusing on what makes you special and celebrating every victory, big or small, you'll find yourself more resilient and ready to face challenges head-on. Keep shining and never forget to give yourself the credit you deserve!

CHAPTER 2

HEALTH AND HYGIENE

Essential Practices for Maintaining Good Health and Hygiene

G et ready to master the art of looking and feeling your best! As a teenager, your body is going through tons of changes, making good health and hygiene more important than ever. But don't stress—this chapter will show you how to stay in top-notch shape without turning it into a chore. From head to toe, we've got you covered with all the tips you need to stay fresh, clean, and healthy, all while having a little fun and laughter along the way.

In this chapter, we'll guide you through establishing a skincare routine that suits your specific skin type. Whether your skin is oily, dry, or a combination, we've got tips and product suggestions to tackle each scenario.

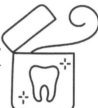

You'll also learn about the importance of daily dental care and regular check-ups, not just for a dazzling smile but for overall health.

We'll dive into menstrual health, discussing different products and how to manage those pesky symptoms. By the end, you'll be armed with practical advice to keep yourself feeling great and looking fabulous.

Establishing a Skincare Routine

Imagine, you're standing in front of a mirror. You might notice your skin shining like a glazed donut or feeling as dry as a desert. Understanding whether your skin is oily, dry, or somewhere in between (also called combination skin) is key to picking out products that will make your face happy and healthy. It's kind of like knowing your shoe size – you wouldn't want to run a marathon in shoes that are too tight or too loose, right? The same goes for skin care!

Let's start with oily skin. It's usually shiny, especially around the forehead, nose, and chin – areas we call the T-zone. There's nothing wrong with a bit of shine, but too much oil can sometimes lead to breakouts. If that sounds like your skin, you'll need products that help keep the oil in check without stripping it completely. Look for words like "oil-free" and "non-comedogenic" on the packaging.

Dry skin, on the other hand, often feels tight, flaky, or itchy. If your skin type sounds like this, think of it as if your face is thirsty - you need moisturizing products that quench its thirst. Ingredients like hyaluronic acid and glycerin are fantastic for locking in moisture and keeping your skin plump and hydrated.

If you've got combination skin, welcome to the club! This means some parts of your face, like the T-zone, might be oily, while others are dry. You'll want to mix and match products to find what works best for the different areas of your skin.

Once you've nailed down your skin type, it's time to talk about routines. Establishing a skincare routine is like setting up a solid game plan for a sports match. You don't just walk onto the field without warming up, right? Your mornings and evenings should have definite steps that set the foundation for healthy skin.

In the morning, start with a gentle cleanser to wash off any oils or sweat from the night. Follow up with a toner to balance your skin's pH levels and prep it for the next steps. Then, go for a serum that targets your specific skin concerns – maybe it's hydration, brightening, or treating acne. Don't forget to moisturize, even if your skin is oily.

At night, you'll want to cleanse again to remove the day's grime. Double cleansing – using an oil-based cleanser followed by a water-based one – can be especially effective. Think of it like double-checking your homework. Follow up with the same steps: toner, serum, and moisturizer. Adding an eye cream can also help keep those under-eye bags at bay.

Now, let's tackle common skin issues like acne and dryness. Acne is like that annoying mosquito bite you just can't help but scratch. Whether it's hormonal or stress-related, pimples are part of life, but they don't have to ruin your day. Look for products containing salicylic acid or benzoyl peroxide, which help to unclog pores and reduce inflammation. Spot treatments can be lifesavers here – dab a little on problem areas before bed, and it can work overnight.

For dryness, layering hydrating products is key. Start with a hydrating toner, then apply a serum with ingredients like hyaluronic acid, and follow up with a rich moisturizer. During colder months, you might want to switch to a heavier cream to combat the effects of the chilly air.

Another hack for handling these issues is not to overdo it. Sometimes less is more. Piling on too many products can overwhelm your skin and make things worse. Stick to a few basics and give them time to work their magic.

And now, the secret superpower: reading labels. Learning to understand skincare labels can feel like decoding a secret message. But once you get the hang of it, you're basically a skincare wizard. Knowing what ingredients to look for and which to avoid can save you a lot of trouble.

Ingredients like parabens, sulfates, and artificial fragrances can be irritating for many people. Instead, look for natural, gentle alternatives. For example, tea tree oil is a great natural alternative to harsher acne treatments. Aloe vera can soothe and hydrate without clogging pores.

Reading labels also helps you become more aware of what exactly you're putting on your skin. It's empowering to know that you have control over what touches your face. Plus, it adds a level of mindfulness to your routine, making it a more intentional and enjoyable practice.

Empower yourself by experimenting with samples. Many skincare brands offer sample sizes, so you can try products without committing to a full-sized version. It's like trying on clothes before you buy them. This way, you can figure out what works best for you without ending up with a drawer full of products that just aren't doing it for your skin.

Importance of Dental Care and Regular Check-ups

Alright, girls, let's talk teeth! Believe it or not, maintaining good dental hygiene isn't just about having a dazzling smile for those selfies. It's crucial for your overall health. So, buckle up; we're diving into the world of toothbrushes and dentists.

First off, daily dental hygiene practices. This might sound like a no-brainer, but proper brushing and flossing techniques are super important. You know that whole "brush your teeth twice a day" thing? It's actually legit. But don't just brush for the sake of brushing; make sure you're doing it right. Tilt your toothbrush at a 45-degree angle to your gums and use gentle, circular motions. And don't forget to brush for two full minutes—yes, a whole two minutes! You can even hum a song in your head to keep track.

Flossing is another key player in this game. Yes, it's kind of a hassle, but sliding that tiny string between your teeth removes food particles and plaque that your toothbrush can't reach. Think of flossing as giving your teeth a little hug—clearing out the gunk that could eventually lead to cavities or gum disease. Do it once a day, preferably before bedtime.

Now let's chat about why regular check-ups with your dentist matter. I know, I know, visiting the dentist might feel like torture. The scraping, the poking... Not fun. But these visits are essential for catching issues before they become major problems. Think of your dentist as a tooth detective. They can spot cavities, gum disease, or even signs of oral cancer early on, which makes treatment easier and more effective. Plus, during these visits, you usually get your teeth professionally cleaned. Say goodbye to stubborn plaque and hello to a squeaky clean mouth!

Speaking of keeping your mouth clean, did you know that what you eat affects your dental health too? Yep, nutrition plays a big role. Foods rich in calcium and phosphorus, like cheese, almonds, and leafy greens, can strengthen your teeth. Chewing crunchy fruits and vegetables, like apples and carrots, stimulates saliva production. Saliva is nature's defense against cavities because it washes away food particles and neutralizes acids in your mouth.

Avoiding sugary snacks and drinks is also key. Bacteria in your mouth love sugar, and they turn it into acid that erodes your enamel, the protective outer layer of your teeth. So, if you've got a sweet tooth, try to limit your intake and always rinse your mouth with water afterward. If you do indulge in something sugary, consider chewing sugar-free gum afterward to increase saliva flow and help clean your teeth.

Alright, now what happens if you face some common dental issues like sensitivity, cavities, or need orthodontic care? No worries, you've got this. Let's break it down. Sensitivity often comes from exposed dentin, the layer under your enamel, making your teeth react to hot, cold, or sweet foods and drinks. Switching to a toothpaste designed for sensitive teeth can really help. These toothpastes have compounds that block the pathways to the nerves of your teeth.

Now, about cavities—they suck, but they're pretty common. Cavities form when enamel gets worn away by bacteria-produced acid. If you suspect you have one (think persistent toothache or visible holes), get to your dentist pronto. They'll likely fill the cavity, which stops it from getting bigger and causing more pain.

And orthodontics... maybe your dentist has hinted that braces or aligners could be in your future. Orthodontic treatment isn't just about achieving a picture-perfect smile. Crooked or misaligned teeth can make cleaning harder, leading to an increased risk of cavities and gum disease. Braces or clear aligners gradually straighten your teeth, making them easier to clean and healthier overall. So, while wearing braces might feel like forever, the results are totally worth it.

Daily Hygiene Routine

From Morning to Night

Feeling great and looking fabulous starts with a solid daily hygiene routine. Think of it as your personal care checklist that sets you up for success every single day. Let's break it down step-by-step so you can breeze through your routine and face the day with confidence.

Morning Routine: Wake Up and Shine!

1. **Face Care:** Now you know that you need to start your day by washing your face with a gentle cleanser. Remember, this removes any oils or sweat that accumulated while you slept. Pat your face dry with a clean towel, then apply a toner to balance your skin's pH levels. Follow up with a light moisturizer to keep your skin hydrated.

2. **Oral Care:** After cleansing your face, it's time to brush your teeth. Remember to use a fluoride toothpaste and a soft-bristled toothbrush. Brush for at least two minutes, making sure to reach every surface of your teeth. Don't forget to brush your tongue too, as it can harbor bacteria. Finish off with flossing to remove any food particles between your teeth and rinse with mouthwash for extra freshness.

3. **Body Care:** A quick shower in the morning can help wake you up and leave you feeling fresh. And make it fun! Choose a scented body wash that you love and focus on areas that sweat more, like your underarms. Rinse off and dry thoroughly. Apply deodorant or antiperspirant to keep body odor at bay throughout the day. If you have dry skin, use a light body lotion after your shower to lock in moisture.

4. **Hair Care:** Depending on your hair type, you might wash your hair daily or every few days. Use a shampoo and conditioner suitable for your hair type—oily, dry, or normal. Gently towel-dry your hair and use a wide-tooth comb to detangle it. Avoid using too much heat from blow dryers or styling tools, which can damage your hair over time.

Midday Freshen-Up: Staying Fresh on the Go

1. **Hand Hygiene:** Throughout the day, keep your hands clean by washing them regularly, especially before eating and after using the restroom. Carry a small bottle of hand sanitizer for those times when soap and water aren't available.

2. **Face Touch-Ups:** If your skin tends to get oily, carry blotting papers or oil-absorbing sheets to dab away excess shine without ruining your makeup. A quick touch-up can keep you feeling confident all day long.

3. **Breath Check:** Keep mints or sugar-free gum handy to freshen your breath after meals. A quick rinse with water can also help wash away food particles.

Evening Routine: Wind Down and Refresh

1. **Face Care:** In the evening, it's essential to remove any makeup and cleanse your skin. Use a gentle cleanser to wash away the day's dirt, oil, and makeup. If you wear makeup, consider double cleansing—first with an oil-based cleanser to break down makeup, then with a water-based cleanser to clean your skin. Follow up with a toner, serum, and a richer moisturizer to hydrate your skin overnight.

2. **Oral Care:** Brush your teeth again before bed, using the same technique as in the morning. Floss to remove any remaining food particles and use mouthwash to help kill bacteria and freshen your breath. This bedtime routine keeps your teeth strong and your breath fresh.

3. **Body Care:** A quick shower before bed can help you relax and wash away the day's sweat and grime. If you prefer not to shower twice a day, simply washing your face, hands, and feet can make a big difference in how fresh you feel.

4. **Hair Care:** Brush your hair to remove tangles and distribute natural oils. If you plan to wash your hair in the morning, consider using a satin or silk pillowcase to reduce friction and prevent hair breakage while you sleep.

Wrapping Up: Your Daily Hygiene Routine

By sticking to a daily hygiene routine, you're not just taking care of your body—you're building habits that will serve you for a lifetime. Each step you take is an act of self-care, showing yourself and the world that you matter. So go ahead, embrace your routine, and enjoy the feeling of being clean, confident, and ready to take on anything!

Understanding Menstrual Health and Hygiene Products

Alright, let's dive into the wonderful world of menstrual health! If you're a teenage girl, chances are you've either just started your period or it's right around the corner. And it's okay to feel a mix of curiosity, confusion, and maybe even dread about it. But don't worry – we're here to help you navigate through this natural part of life like a pro.

First up, let's talk about the basics of the menstrual cycle. Your menstrual cycle is essentially the monthly series of changes your body goes through to prepare for a potential pregnancy. Sounds intense, right? But here's the low-down: The average cycle lasts about 28-30 days but don't stress if yours is a bit shorter or longer. It kicks off with menstruation, which is when you'll actually have your period. This can last anywhere from 3 to 7 days. During this time, your uterus sheds its lining because no pregnancy has occurred. After your period ends, your body gets back to work preparing for the next cycle. Ovulation typically happens around the middle of the cycle – that's when an egg is released from one of your ovaries. If the egg isn't fertilized, boom, the cycle repeats itself.

Now, let's move on to the actual products you'll use during your period. There are a few different options, and it might take trying out a couple to see what works best for you.

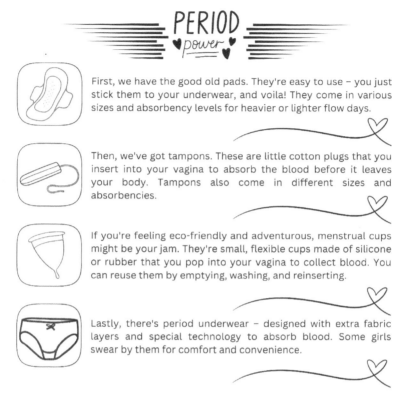

First, we have the good old pads. They're easy to use – you just stick them to your underwear, and voila! They come in various sizes and absorbency levels for heavier or lighter flow days.

Then, we've got tampons. These are little cotton plugs that you insert into your vagina to absorb the blood before it leaves your body. Tampons also come in different sizes and absorbencies.

If you're feeling eco-friendly and adventurous, menstrual cups might be your jam. They're small, flexible cups made of silicone or rubber that you pop into your vagina to collect blood. You can reuse them by emptying, washing, and reinserting.

Lastly, there's period underwear – designed with extra fabric layers and special technology to absorb blood. Some girls swear by them for comfort and convenience.

Cramps, mood swings, and bloating. Oh my! These pesky symptoms can be the worst part of having your period. But, lucky for you, there are ways to manage them. Let's start with cramps. Exercising might be the furthest thing from your mind when you're curled up in pain, but light activities like walking or yoga can help alleviate cramps by increasing blood flow. Applying heat to your lower abdomen with a heating pad or hot water bottle can also soothe those muscles. Over-the-counter pain relievers like ibuprofen can be really effective too; just make sure you follow the recommended dosage. For mood swings, keep in mind that you're not alone – lots of girls experience emotional ups and downs due to hormonal fluctuations. Try to maintain a balanced diet, get plenty of sleep, and find healthy ways to cope with stress, like journaling or talking to a friend. Drinking water can help reduce bloating as well, so stay hydrated!

Talking about periods may feel a little awkward or embarrassing, but starting conversations about menstrual health with your peers and family can be empowering and super helpful. It's good to share tips and experiences with friends – chances are, they're dealing with the same stuff you are. Don't hesitate to ask your mom, sister, or another trusted adult about their experiences and advice. Building these conversations helps normalize menstruation and makes it less of a taboo topic. Plus, it can be a great bonding experience. You could even consider creating a 'period kit' with essentials like pads, tampons, pain relievers, and chocolate – just in case anyone needs it.

Nutritional Tips for Balanced Meals

Alright, girls, let's dive into the world of nutrition! Ever wondered why everyone makes such a big deal about what we eat? Well, it's because good nutrition can seriously up your game when it comes to feeling awesome and staying healthy. So let's break it all down, step by step.

Understanding Nutritional Basics

First things first, let's talk macronutrients and micronutrients. Don't worry, it's not as scary as it sounds. Macronutrients are your carbs, proteins, and fats—basically, the stuff that gives you energy and keeps you going throughout the day. Carbs (carbohydrates) are like the fuel for your body. Think of them as the gas in your car.

They're found in foods like bread, rice, pasta, fruits, and veggies. Proteins are the building blocks of your muscles and tissues. You can find them in meat, fish, eggs, beans, and nuts. Fats, despite their bad rap, are super important too—they help with brain function, hormone production, and absorbing vitamins. Healthy fats can be found in avocado, olive oil, nuts, and fatty fish.

Now, onto micronutrients which include vitamins and minerals. These guys don't provide energy per se, but they are essential for everything from strong bones (hello, calcium!) to maintaining a healthy immune system (vitamin C, anyone?). You get these nutrients from a variety of fruits, vegetables, dairy products, and even meats. Eating a colorful plate is not just pretty but also nutritious!

Creating Balanced Meals

So, how do you put this knowledge into action? Let's look at balanced meals. Imagine your plate divided into sections. Half of your plate should be filled with fruits and veggies—they're packed with fiber, vitamins, and minerals. Aim for a mix of colors, like bell peppers, carrots, spinach, and berries. One-quarter of your plate should be dedicated to protein. This could be chicken, tofu, beans, or fish. The remaining quarter is for grains, preferably whole grains like brown rice, quinoa, or whole wheat bread.

For example, a balanced dinner could be grilled chicken, steamed broccoli, a side salad with mixed greens, and a serving of quinoa. Or maybe a veggie stir-fry with tofu and brown rice. It's all about variety and ensuring you're getting a little bit of everything your body needs to thrive.

Healthy Snacking Choices

Now, let's tackle snacks. We all get those mid-afternoon munchies, right? Instead of reaching for chips or candy, think about snacks that give you energy and keep you full until your next meal. Fruits like apples, bananas, or grapes are great options. Pair them with a handful of almonds or a spoonful of peanut butter for some added protein.

Yogurt with a sprinkle of granola is another fab choice. How about carrot sticks or cucumber slices with hummus? Yum! The idea is to combine different food groups so you get a mix of nutrients and stay satisfied longer. Keep a stash of these goodies handy, whether you're at school, doing homework, or hanging out with friends.

Hydration Importance

Last but definitely not least, let's chat about hydration. Your body is around 60% water, so keeping hydrated is crucial for everything from glowing skin to better concentration. How much water do you need? A general rule is eight 8-ounce glasses a day, but more if you're active or it's particularly hot outside.

Water is obviously the best choice for staying hydrated, but not the only one. Herbal teas, milk, and water-rich fruits and veggies (like watermelon and cucumber) can also contribute to your daily intake.

Try carrying a reusable water bottle with you so you can sip throughout the day, and jazz it up with slices of lemon, lime, or mint leaves if plain water isn't your thing.

And hey, if you're not a fan of gulping down glass after glass, you can make it fun! Challenge yourself and your friends to see who can drink the most water in a day. Spoiler: everyone wins because staying hydrated is a game-changer.

Conclusion

Embrace the Power of Good Hygiene

By now, you've learned that maintaining good health and hygiene is more than just a daily routine—it's a way of life that empowers you to feel confident and stay healthy. From understanding your skin type to mastering the art of dental care, each practice helps you take control of your well-being. As you navigate through these exciting and sometimes challenging teenage years, remember that taking care of your body is a form of self-respect and self-love.

Good hygiene habits, like any other habits, might take a bit of time to develop, but once they're part of your daily routine, they'll feel as natural as breathing. Whether it's sticking to your skincare routine, flossing before bed, or staying hydrated, these small, consistent actions add up to big benefits. So, keep exploring what works best for you, listen to your body, and enjoy the process of discovering your unique path to health and happiness.

Remember, you are worth the time and effort it takes to look after yourself. Keep shining, keep smiling, and keep rocking your way through these incredible years. You've got this!

CHAPTER 3

COOKING AND NUTRITION

Essential Culinary Skills and Healthy Eating Habits for Teenage Girls

Imagine confidently striding into the kitchen, ready to create delicious meals without the fear of burning toast or cutting your fingers—sounds amazing, right? Mastering essential culinary skills and embracing healthy eating habits can be a total game-changer for any teenage girl looking to rule the kitchen. With the right know-how, whipping up nutritious meals becomes not just possible but incredibly satisfying. In this chapter, you'll learn how to handle the kitchen's sharpest tools like a pro, making every mealtime a breeze and turning you into a culinary star!

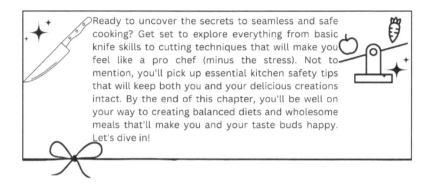

Ready to uncover the secrets to seamless and safe cooking? Get set to explore everything from basic knife skills to cutting techniques that will make you feel like a pro chef (minus the stress). Not to mention, you'll pick up essential kitchen safety tips that will keep both you and your delicious creations intact. By the end of this chapter, you'll be well on your way to creating balanced diets and wholesome meals that'll make you and your taste buds happy. Let's dive in!

Basic Knife Skills and Kitchen Safety

Understanding how to handle knives properly and incorporating essential kitchen safety tips is vital for building confidence while cooking. It's not just about avoiding accidents but feeling like you can tackle any recipe that comes your way. Let's dive into these important skills.

First off, let's talk knives. Knowing the right knife for each task can make a world of difference. Imagine trying to chop a carrot with a tiny paring knife – not fun, right? Each knife in your kitchen has a special job to do. The chef's knife, for example, is perfect for most of your chopping needs, while the serrated knife is your go-to for slicing bread. And then there's the paring knife, best for smaller tasks like peeling or slicing small fruits. Using the right knife not only makes the job easier but also safer. When you're not struggling with the wrong tool, you're less likely to slip and cut yourself.

Now, on to developing safe cutting techniques. Have you ever seen professional chefs chopping away at lightning speed? While you don't need to slice like a pro, adopting some of their techniques can boost your confidence.

One key method is the claw grip. Instead of holding your food with your fingers splayed out, tuck your fingertips under and use your knuckles as a guide for the knife. This keeps your fingers safely out of the knife's path. Practice makes perfect here. Start slow and gradually pick up speed as you become more comfortable.

Beyond just how you hold the knife, consider how you stand and move. It might sound silly, but having a firm stance with your feet shoulder-width apart can give you better control and stability. Also, make sure your cutting board isn't slipping around – place a damp towel underneath to keep it steady. A stable work surface is half the battle won when it comes to safely using knives.

Once you've finished cutting, where do those knives go? Organizing knives in designated areas decreases the likelihood of accidents. You don't want someone rummaging through a drawer and accidentally grabbing a sharp blade. Knife blocks or magnetic strips are perfect for this. They keep knives accessible but safely out of the way. Plus, storing knives properly ensures they stay sharp longer, and a sharp knife is actually safer. It's less likely to slip than a dull one, giving you cleaner cuts without extra pressure.

Let's not forget about cleaning knives properly. Always wash them by hand – no tossing them in the dishwasher! The high temperatures and harsh detergents can damage the blade and handle. Use warm, soapy water and a dishcloth, cleaning from the spine down to avoid accidental nicks. Dry them immediately after washing to prevent rust and store them in their designated spot.

Now, beyond knives, understanding general kitchen safety is crucial. Fire safety, for instance, can't be overlooked. Kitchens have open flames, hot surfaces, and lots of flammable items. Always keep a fire extinguisher nearby and know how to use it. If you're working with oil and it catches fire, never throw water on it – that'll only make things worse. Cover the pan with a lid to smother the flames or use baking soda if it's a small fire.

While we're talking about heat, always use oven mitts or pot holders when handling anything hot. Sounds obvious, right? But you'd be surprised how easy it is to forget in the middle of a busy cooking session. Also, make a habit of turning pot handles inward on the stove. This simple tip prevents them from being knocked off, especially if there are younger siblings running around.

Let's touch on a few more handy tips. Ever thought about what to do if you spill something on the floor? Clean it up right away to avoid slips and falls. Wear non-slip shoes if possible, especially if you're standing for long periods. And don't forget to keep pets out of the kitchen while you cook – not only can they trip you up, but certain foods can be harmful to them.

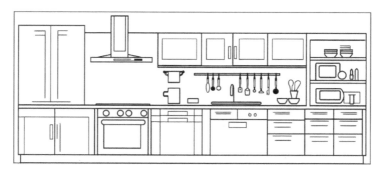

Lastly, organization isn't just for knives. Keeping your workspace tidy reduces clutter and distractions. Know where your ingredients and tools are so you're not scrambling to find things mid-recipe. Developing a habit of cleaning as you go means you'll have a spotless kitchen by the time you finish cooking – double win!

Simple, Nutritious Recipes to Start With

What if you could start your day not just with a smile but with the energy you need to conquer it? Nutritious breakfasts are like the secret weapon for any teenage girl. They don't just taste good—they power up your brain and body for all that school work, sports, and socializing you've got going on. Let's talk breakfast ideas: think smoothies packed with fruits and a scoop of Greek yogurt, or avocado toast sprinkled with a little sea salt and chili flakes. And who could say no to a fun smoothie bowl topped with granola and fresh berries? The goal is to mix it up and keep it exciting so you actually look forward to breakfast each morning.

Moving on to lunches, why settle for the same old cafeteria food when you can whip up something delicious right at home? Preparing lunches isn't just about the food—it's a chance to take control of what you're putting into your body. Try making a colorful veggie wrap with hummus, or maybe a quinoa salad with cherry tomatoes, cucumber, and feta cheese. You can even throw in some grilled chicken for extra protein. Homemade lunches are a great way to avoid the pitfalls of fast food and vending machine snacks, ensuring you're getting fresh ingredients and balanced nutrition.

Creating balanced meals teaches you skills that will serve you well beyond your teenage years. Imagine knowing how to prepare a dinner that's both yummy and nutritious without having to rely on takeout menus. It's easier than you think! Picture this: grilled salmon with a side of roasted vegetables and maybe a quinoa pilaf. Not only are you cooking something wonderful, but you're also learning which foods work well together to give you a complete meal. These skills will make you more independent and confident in the kitchen, setting you up for a future where you can easily whip up a meal without breaking a sweat.

Then there's the beauty of being flexible in cooking. You know, life doesn't always go as planned. Maybe you wanted to make spaghetti carbonara but realized you're out of eggs. No problem! This is where adaptability and resourcefulness come into play. Learning to substitute ingredients can make cooking an adventure rather than a chore. If you're out of eggs, try using a splash of cream or a bit of butter. Missing tomatoes? How about some roasted peppers instead? Each time you adjust, you become more comfortable with thinking on your feet—and who knows, you might even invent a new favorite dish!

It's important to remember that cooking should be fun and flexible. You don't have to stick to rigid recipes; feel free to experiment and see what works best for you. Maybe you'll find that you love adding a bit of cinnamon to your morning oatmeal or prefer your salads with a splash of lemon juice. This freedom to play around makes cooking less of a task and more of an enjoyable part of your daily routine.

Getting Started with Easy, Healthy Recipes

Ready to put those skills to use? Let's start with some simple, healthy recipes that are perfect for beginners:

1. Overnight Oats

Mix 1/2 cup of rolled oats, 1/2 cup of almond milk, 1 tablespoon of chia seeds, and a drizzle of honey in a jar. Leave it in the fridge overnight, and in the morning, top it with fresh fruit like berries or banana slices for a delicious, ready-to-eat breakfast.

2. Veggie Wrap

Take a whole-grain tortilla and spread a layer of hummus over it. Add a handful of spinach leaves, shredded carrots, sliced bell peppers, and a sprinkle of feta cheese. Roll it up, and you have a quick, healthy lunch that's perfect for school or on the go.

3. Easy Stir-Fry

In a hot skillet, sauté sliced bell peppers, broccoli florets, and snap peas with a bit of olive oil and minced garlic. Add in cubed tofu or chicken pieces, and stir in a simple sauce made of soy sauce, honey, and a pinch of red pepper flakes. Serve over brown rice or noodles for a nutritious dinner.

4. Smoothie Bowl

Blend together a frozen banana, a handful of spinach, a cup of frozen berries, and a splash of almond milk until smooth. Pour the smoothie into a bowl and top with granola, chia seeds, and sliced strawberries for a fun and healthy breakfast or snack.

These recipes are just the beginning. As you gain confidence in the kitchen, you'll find that creating healthy, delicious meals can be both simple and rewarding. So go ahead, put on your apron, and get cooking!

Inspiration can come from anywhere, whether it's cookbooks, online recipes, or even family traditions. Feel free to put your spin on things. Like the idea of making lasagna? Why not try a veggie-packed version with zucchini and spinach? Love tacos? Mix it up with fish or even a plant-based filling.

The main takeaway here is that cooking is an awesome skill to have, and it doesn't have to be complicated. Start with simple recipes, focus on fresh ingredients, and before you know it, you'll be dishing out meals that are not only healthy but a delight to eat. Breakfasts, lunches, dinners—all contributing to a balanced diet that fuels your body and mind.

Reading and Understanding Nutrition Labels

Alright, let's talk about deciphering those mysterious nutrition labels you see on food packages and how that can help you make awesome, healthy choices. First up, understanding serving sizes is a game-changer for controlling portions. You know how you can flip over a bag of chips and it says "serving size: 10 chips," but who stops at just ten chips? Getting the hang of what a proper serving looks like helps you understand how much you're actually eating versus what you think you're eating. So next time you're munching away, take a peek at that serving size, and you'll be ahead of the game in portion control.

Now, let's dive into nutrient functions. It might sound boring, but trust me, knowing what nutrients do for your body is super cool and useful. For example, proteins are the building blocks of your muscles, while carbs give you energy to crush it during soccer practice or dance class. Recognizing these roles means you can balance your diet more effectively. Not sure if you're getting enough iron? Check that nutrition label! Understanding what's in your food helps you ensure you're getting a well-rounded mix of everything your body needs to function at its best.

Moving on to ingredient sourcing, ever wonder why some products boast "100% whole grain" or "organic"? Ingredients matter a ton when it comes to health choices. Knowing where your food comes from and what's in it can help you steer clear of things like too many preservatives or artificial ingredients, which aren't great for your body. Plus, sometimes brands use sneaky names to hide less-than-healthy ingredients. Being able to spot these can make a huge difference in your overall health.

So, okay, you've got some solid info now, but what do you do with it? Well, these skills aren't just for show—they empower you to become a savvy shopper. Imagine going to the grocery store and being able to pick out foods that are not only delicious but nutritious too. You'll know to look at the sugar content in that cereal box before tossing it in the cart or check for trans fats in your favorite snack. This way, learning these skills makes grocery shopping a breeze and ensures you're making choices that nourish your body.

Back to serving sizes for a moment—this truly deserves extra attention because it's such a crucial part of healthy eating. Have you ever looked at a bottle of soda and seen that it has "2.5 servings"? That means if you drink the whole bottle, you're consuming more calories and sugar than you might have realized. By understanding serving sizes, you can better control your intake, avoid overeating, and keep everything balanced. Think of it as mastering the art of measuring without the actual measuring!

And let's not forget how vital it is to comprehend the functions of different nutrients. Each nutrient plays a unique role in maintaining our health and vitality. For instance, calcium is essential for strong bones and teeth, vitamin C boosts your immune system, and fiber aids digestion. Understanding these functions allows you to tailor your meals to meet your specific health needs. Are you feeling sluggish? Maybe you need more protein-rich foods like beans or chicken. Feeling rundown? Reach for that orange or spinach salad rich in vitamins.

The source of your food is another area that shouldn't be underestimated. Food labels often mention whether something is non-GMO (non-genetically modified organisms), organic, or sustainably sourced. These terms aren't just buzzwords—they signify quality and health benefits. Organic foods tend to have fewer pesticides and might even offer more nutritional value. By choosing organic or sustainably sourced items, you're not just benefiting yourself but also supporting practices that are good for the environment. It's a win-win!

Speaking of wise decision-making, how about some practical application? When you learn to read and understand nutrition labels, meal planning becomes significantly easier. You can whip up a week's worth of balanced meals without second-guessing yourself. Picture this: you're at the supermarket, eyeing two different jars of peanut butter. One jar contains added sugars and hydrogenated oils, while the other lists simple, natural ingredients. With your newly acquired skills, you'd naturally opt for the healthier choice. Shopping becomes a reflection of your commitment to a balanced and nutritious diet.

Okay, let's recount a fun story to bring this home. Imagine you and your friends are throwing a movie night. You head to the store to grab snacks. Equipped with your knowledge of nutrition labels, you navigate the aisles like a pro. Instead of grabbing the usual suspects loaded with unhealthy fats and sugars, you choose air-popped popcorn, hummus with veggie sticks, and maybe some dark chocolate. Your friends are surprised but love the snacks—and you feel great knowing you made healthy choices!

But wait, there's more. Deciphering nutrition labels isn't just about avoiding the bad stuff; it's also about embracing the good. Foods packed with essential nutrients can boost your overall mood, energy levels, and even mental clarity. By routinely making informed food choices, you set yourself up for long-term health benefits. It's like giving your future self a giant high-five!

 So next time you're standing in front of that wall of granola bars, don't just reach for the one with the prettiest packaging. Take a moment to flip it over and read the label. Check for hidden sugars, unhealthy fats, and artificial additives. Look for high fiber content, natural sweeteners, and wholesome ingredients. The more you practice, the more second nature it will become.

Creating a Weekly Meal Plan

Planning balanced meals can seem like a daunting task, especially when juggling school, extracurricular activities, and social life. But improving organization can surprisingly reduce stress levels while grocery shopping and cooking. Picture this: It's Friday evening, and you're staring at an empty fridge, unsure of what to make for dinner. If you had a meal plan, you wouldn't be in this pickle! Allocating a small chunk of time each week to plan your meals can prevent these last-minute scrambles and make your culinary adventures much smoother.

Now, let's talk about assessing dietary needs and preferences—this is where you get to take the reins on your nutrition journey. Think about what you enjoy eating and how you feel after different meals. Do you need more energy throughout the day? Or maybe you're looking to incorporate more veggies into your diet? Taking the time to understand your nutritional requirements makes it easier to create meals that genuinely benefit you. This not only enhances your well-being but also inspires a sense of ownership over your health. Plus, it's super empowering to know exactly what goes into fueling your body.

Creating a structured list before you head out for groceries is another game-changer. How many times have you gone to grab "just one thing" and ended up with a cart full of snacks? Yeah, we've all been there. A well-thought-out list helps keep those impulse buys in check, saving money and reducing food waste. You'll find it much easier to stick to your budget and avoid those sneaky bags of chips that somehow always end up in the cart.

Let's dive into batch cooking—your new best friend. Imagine whipping up several meals in one go and freeing up precious time for other activities during the week. Not only does batch cooking simplify weekly cooking, but it also ensures you have nutritious meals ready to go, even on the busiest days. Instead of resorting to fast food or instant noodles, you've got healthy options lined up. Batch cooking can mean making a big pot of spaghetti sauce, soup, or even pre-cooking grains like rice and quinoa. Store them in portion-sized containers, and voila! You've just unlocked more free time without compromising on healthy eating.

So, how do you start planning these balanced meals? Begin by jotting down some of your favorite recipes. Ensure they include a mix of proteins, carbs, and fats to give your body the balanced diet it needs. Next, map out your week—what nights are busy, which days you might have more time to cook, and so on. Once you have a basic outline, fill in your meal ideas accordingly.

Shopping smartly is the next step. Stick to the perimeter of the store where fresh produce, meats, and dairy products are typically found. The middle aisles often house processed foods that we want to limit. With your structured list in hand, you'll breeze through the store in no time, knowing exactly what you need and avoiding unnecessary purchases.

And let's not forget about variety. Eating the same meals every week can get dull pretty quickly. Mix things up by trying new recipes or experimenting with different cuisines. Not only does this make mealtimes exciting, but it also exposes you to a wider range of nutrients.

When it comes to batch cooking, consider investing in good-quality storage containers. They'll keep your meals fresh and make it easy to grab and go. Also, don't be afraid to double or triple recipes. You'd be surprised how easy it is to prepare larger quantities of food with just a little extra effort.

Additionally, getting into the habit of prepping ingredients ahead of time can be extremely helpful. Washing, chopping, and storing vegetables in advance significantly cuts down on meal prep time during the week. Plus, having everything ready to go makes cooking less daunting and way more efficient.

Remember, the goal here is to create a plan that works for you. If you try something and it doesn't quite fit, tweak it until it does. Maybe you prefer prepping lunches instead of dinners, or perhaps you find doing a mid-week mini meal prep session suits your schedule better. Whatever keeps you consistent and makes healthy eating less of a chore is worth exploring.

Finally, don't beat yourself up if things don't go perfectly from the start. Planning balanced meals is a skill, and like any other skill, it gets better with practice. Some weeks will be flawless, others might be a bit rocky—and that's totally okay. The important thing is that you're putting in the effort to take care of your body.

To sum it all up, improving organization in meal planning reduces stress, makes grocery shopping a breeze, and cuts down on unnecessary spending. Understanding your dietary needs empowers you to make choices that benefit your overall health. Creating a structured list keeps you focused and minimizes waste. Batch cooking saves time and ensures you always have nutritious meals ready to go. By adopting these practices, you'll find that maintaining a balanced diet is not only manageable but also enjoyable.

Lessons Learned

Alright, so we've covered the basics of knife skills and kitchen safety, ensuring you don't lose a finger while chopping that carrot or burning down the house with a simple stir-fry. With your new culinary powers, not only can you whip up mouth-watering dishes, but you'll also do it with grace and zero injuries. Plus, getting comfy in the kitchen means you're just a few steps away from creating Instagram-worthy meals that'll make everyone jealous.

Now, blending these awesome knife skills with our nutritious recipes, you're all set to conquer breakfast, lunch, and dinner like a pro. You've got the know-how to prepare balanced meals, understand nutrition labels, and even plan a week's worth of deliciousness. So go ahead, channel your inner chef, and remember—cooking should be fun and flexible. Experiment, enjoy the process, and before you know it, you'll be a kitchen superstar, impressing everyone with your newfound skills and tasty creations!

Chapter 4

Cleaning and Organization

Cleaning and Organization

Cleaning and keeping your space organized may not sound like the most exciting thing in the world, but trust me, it's a game-changer. Imagine waking up every day to a room that looks straight out of a Pinterest board—no clutter on the floors, bed neatly made, everything in its place. Not only does a clean environment boost your productivity, but it also creates a sense of well-being. You'll be surprised at how much more relaxed and focused you feel when you're not surrounded by chaos. So, buckle up because we're taking a fun ride through the land of cleanliness and organization!

In this chapter, we'll dive into practical methods for maintaining a tidy living space effortlessly. We'll start with daily cleaning routines for the bedroom, bathroom, kitchen, and living room—places where mess can sneak up on you quickly. You'll learn simple hacks like making your bed first thing in the morning, wiping down bathroom surfaces, and loading the dishwasher right after meals. We'll also discuss how to turn these tasks into habits with tips like setting reminders on your phone or creating a checklist. Whether you're aiming to keep your study area spotless or trying to transform your wardrobe into a functional, easy-to-navigate space, this chapter has got you covered. And don't worry, we'll keep things light and fun along the way!

Daily Cleaning Routines for Different Areas

Establishing a daily cleaning routine is like finding your own personal superhero cape. It might not be the most glamorous habit, but it packs a punch in keeping your space consistently clean and making you feel like you've got life all figured out. Let's dive into some easy-peasy ways to make cleaning a no-brainer.

Let's start with the bedroom. Imagine waking up and seeing your bed neatly made—it instantly makes your room look more organized and gives you that "I've-got-my-life-together" vibe. Making your bed daily isn't just about appearances; it sets a positive tone for the rest of your day. It's a small win first thing in the morning, and who doesn't love starting their day with a win? Plus, it only takes a couple of minutes, so no excuses!

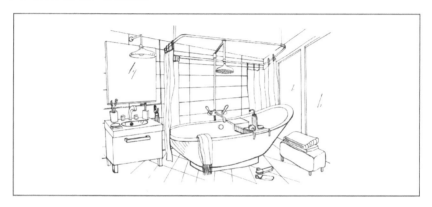

Next up, the bathroom. After brushing your teeth or washing your face, take a few seconds to wipe down the surfaces. This simple act can prevent the buildup of grime and bacteria. Think of it as giving your bathroom a mini spa treatment every day. And let's be real—nobody enjoys scrubbing a week's worth of toothpaste off the sink! By wiping down surfaces daily, you save yourself from those deep-cleaning marathons that nobody looks forward to. Just a quick swipe after each use keeps everything sparkling and fresh.

Now, let's wander over to the kitchen. The kitchen is often the heart of the home, where everyone gathers for meals and snacks. But it can also be the biggest source of chaos if dishes pile up. Loading the dishwasher right after meals can make a huge difference. It fosters a sense of teamwork and shared responsibility among family members. Imagine this: everyone pitches in, placing their plates and utensils directly into the dishwasher after eating. Not only does it keep the kitchen tidy, but it also encourages a culture of cooperation. Plus, there's something oddly satisfying about hitting the start button on a full dishwasher and knowing the magic of modern appliances will handle the rest.

The living room is another hotspot for both activity and mess. Whether you're binge-watching your favorite shows, doing homework, or hanging out with friends, it's easy for clutter to accumulate. Tidying up the living room daily ensures it's always ready for guests and keeps it an inviting space for family gatherings. Quick tasks like fluffing pillows, folding blankets, and picking up stray items can transform the room in just a few minutes. And, let's be honest, having a clean living room makes those spontaneous dance parties way more fun.

So, how do you turn these daily tasks into lasting habits? It's all about consistency. Start by setting small, achievable goals. Maybe today, you'll focus on just making the bed. Tomorrow, add wiping down the bathroom surfaces. Gradually incorporate each task until they become second nature. You can even create a checklist to help you remember. Stick it on your fridge or bathroom mirror where you'll see it daily. Each time you check off a task, you get a little burst of satisfaction. Plus, checking off lists can be strangely addictive—in the best way possible.

If you struggle with remembering or motivation, consider setting reminders on your phone. A gentle nudge at the same time each day can prompt you to complete your tasks until they become a natural part of your routine. Pairing tasks with specific triggers can also be helpful. For example, make your bed as soon as you get up, wipe down the bathroom sink right after brushing your teeth, load the dishwasher immediately after meals, and straighten up the living room before bed.

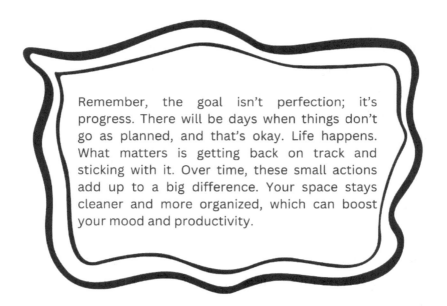

Remember, the goal isn't perfection; it's progress. There will be days when things don't go as planned, and that's okay. Life happens. What matters is getting back on track and sticking with it. Over time, these small actions add up to a big difference. Your space stays cleaner and more organized, which can boost your mood and productivity.

Organizing Your Wardrobe and Study Area

The art of organization is like a secret superpower. It helps you find things quickly, makes your routine smoother, and gives you more time for fun stuff. Let's start with one of the coolest ways to keep your wardrobe organized—sorting clothes by season. Imagine never having to dig through piles of winter sweaters to find your favorite summer dress again. By storing away clothes that are out of season, you free up a lot of space. This makes it easy to grab whatever you're in the mood to wear without causing a mini avalanche every time you open your closet.

Think about it: when winter rolls around, pull out all those cozy sweaters and jackets and tuck away your summer dresses and shorts in a storage bin under your bed or on a high shelf. Labeling bins or using clear containers can save you from guessing games later. Not only does this make life easier but also creates a more aesthetically pleasing wardrobe. Stylish and practical? Yes, please!

Next up, let's tackle your study area. Ever tried to focus on homework but got distracted by a chaotic desk? Been there. Keeping supplies like pens, notebooks, and chargers in easily accessible containers can be a game-changer. When everything has its place, you're less likely to get sidetracked looking for that one pen that always seems to disappear just when you need it the most.

Consider getting some cute organizers or even DIY-ing some if you're into crafts. Mason jars, small baskets, or even repurposed shoe boxes can make fantastic supply holders. Stickers, washi tape, or paint can add a personal touch, making your study space as unique as you are. With everything in its place, you'll spend less time searching and more time actually doing what you need to do.

Now, onto digital organization. If your desktop looks like mine used to—with icons strewn everywhere—it's probably time for a digital makeover. Organizing files into folders isn't just for neat freaks; it's a productivity booster. Start by sorting your files into categories like school, photos, music, and so on. Within each category, create subfolders for specific classes, events, or albums. It might take a bit of time initially, but trust me, future you will be so grateful.

For an extra layer of organization, use color-coding or naming conventions. For instance, prefix your homework files with "HW" and class notes with "Notes." Tools like cloud storage can also be handy. You'll thank yourself when you easily find that important document during crunch time.

Lastly, creating an inviting atmosphere for collaboration can foster teamwork and shared efforts effectively. Whether it's for a group project or a creative hangout with friends, setting up a space that encourages collaboration can be super helpful. This could be a comfy corner in your room with a few chairs and a small table, or even just a section of your living room where everyone can gather.

A few things to consider: good lighting, comfortable seating, and minimal distractions. Throw in some snacks, maybe a whiteboard for brainstorming, and you've got yourself a perfect collaboration hub. Make sure the space feels welcoming and inclusive. Adding a personal touch like inspirational quotes or posters can enhance the vibe, making everyone feel at ease and ready to contribute their best ideas.

So, mastering these techniques not only keeps your space neat but also boosts your efficiency and mood. A well-organized environment can make daily routines run smoother, whether you're getting dressed, studying, working digitally, or collaborating with friends. Organization doesn't have to be boring. With a touch of creativity, you can turn it into an enjoyable and rewarding experience, one step at a time.

As you embrace these organizational strategies, remember that it's okay to tweak them to fit your lifestyle. What works for one person might need a bit of adjustment for another. Feel free to experiment and find out what suits you best. There's no one-size-fits-all approach to staying organized, and that's totally fine.

Decluttering Techniques for a Tidy Environment

Imagine this: You're in your room and everything is everywhere. Clothes are on the bed, books on the floor, old papers scattered around. It looks like a tornado hit! Now, picture how awesome it would feel if everything was neat, tidy, and organized. That's where decluttering comes in. Let's dive into some rock-solid methods to help you transform your space from chaos to calm!

First up is the **4-Box Method**. Grab four boxes (or bags) and label them: keep, donate, trash, and relocate. The idea here is super simple – go through your items one by one, deciding which box each item belongs in. If it's something you love and use regularly, it goes in the keep box. If it's something that no longer serves you but could be useful to someone else, pop it in the donate box. Trash is for stuff that's broken or unusable, and relocate is for things that belong somewhere else in your house.

Keep   Donate   Relocate   Trash

Let's say you're sorting through your closet and find a dress that doesn't fit anymore. If it's still in good condition, it goes in the donate box. That stack of old school assignments? Probably heading for the trash box. And your favorite book that somehow ended up under your bed? Relocate that to your bookshelf. Breaking down the job into these four categories makes it way less overwhelming and keeps things organized as you go.

Next, let's talk about the **'One In, One Out'** rule. Here's the deal: For every new item you bring into your space, you have to get rid of one existing item. Got a new pair of shoes? Then it's time to say goodbye to an older pair. This keeps your belongings from multiplying uncontrollably and makes you think twice before making impulse purchases.

Imagine you just bought a super cute new top. Before hanging it in your closet, take a look at what's already there. Maybe there's a shirt you haven't worn in ages. By following the 'One In, One Out' rule, you'll place the new top in your closet and move the old shirt to the donate box. This not only helps control clutter but also ensures that you truly value everything you own.

Now, let's tackle the **Time-Block Decluttering method.** The idea here is to set a timer for a short period, like 10 minutes, and see how much you can accomplish in that time. This works wonders for those moments when you feel too overwhelmed to start a big cleaning project. Ten minutes is totally doable, right?

You can make it fun by turning it into a game. Put on your favorite playlist, set the timer, and race against the clock to tidy up. Focus on one small area – maybe your desk or a corner of your room. When the timer goes off, stop. You'd be amazed at how much progress you can make in just ten minutes a day. This way, cleaning doesn't feel like a huge chore, and over time you'll see significant improvements in your space.

Lastly, let's chat about **Seasonal Decluttering.** This method aligns your decluttering efforts with the changing seasons. Think spring cleaning, but for all seasons. When the weather changes, it's a great reminder to go through your belongings and freshen up your space.

For example, as summer turns to fall, pack away your summer clothes and bring out your cozy sweaters and scarves. While doing this, consider if there are any summer items you didn't wear and could donate. Maybe there's a swimsuit that's seen better days – time for the trash. As winter approaches, do the same with your fall wardrobe, and so on. This keeps your living space current, functional, and downright pleasant year-round.

By incorporating these decluttering methods into your routine, you can create a space that feels light, clear, and peaceful. It's not just about having a clean room; it's about creating an environment that supports your well-being. When you walk into an organized space, it's easier to focus, relax, and feel good.

These strategies aren't just powerful for improving physical spaces – they can also positively impact your mental state. A clean space often equals a clear mind. Think about how amazing it will feel to invite friends over without worrying about mess or, better yet, waking up to a space that inspires rather than stresses you out.

Maintaining Cleanliness During Busy Periods

When life seems like it's moving at a million miles per hour, maintaining an organized space can feel like an impossible mission. But guess what? It's totally doable! Even with a packed schedule, you can keep your living area in check and stay chill about it. First things first: let's talk priorities.

It's easy to get overwhelmed when you look around and see chaos everywhere. So, start small. Identify the essential areas that need attention first. Is your desk a disaster zone that makes homework feel even more dreadful? Or maybe your closet is overflowing, making it hard to find anything to wear? Focus on these key spots. By tackling the highest priority areas, you create quick wins that motivate you to keep going. Plus, your space starts looking better without feeling like an endless chore.

Now, here's a super handy hack: set a timer for five minutes. Yup, just five minutes. This little trick makes cleaning way less daunting. Instead of thinking you need to spend hours tidying up, commit to just five minutes. You'll be surprised how much you can accomplish in such a short time. Pick up clothes, throw away trash, or organize your desk. The key is consistency. These mini cleanups add up over time, making a big difference without eating into your busy schedule.

Next, let's talk planning. Ever heard of a cleaning calendar? It's basically a lifesaver. Structure some time each week specifically for cleaning tasks. Maybe Monday is 'desk day' and Thursday is 'closet day.' By scheduling cleaning slots, you're less likely to ignore them. It helps transform cleaning from something you dread into a regular habit. You wouldn't skip out on hanging with friends because it's planned, right? Think of cleaning as a date with your future self—a favor you'll thank yourself for later.

But let's be real—life doesn't always go as planned. Sometimes you're swamped with homework, or maybe you just don't feel like cleaning today. And that's okay. Understanding that not every day can be perfect is crucial. Give yourself a break now and then. Recognizing that messiness is part of a busy life reduces a lot of self-imposed pressure. The goal isn't perfection; it's progress.

Alright, now back to prioritizing tasks. Here's a guideline to help you understand what should be cleaned first when you're tight on time. Start by making a list of all the messy spots in your room. Rank them from most to least important based on how often you use them and how their cleanliness affects your mood or productivity. Tackle the top three first. For example, if your study area is where you spend the most time, make it your number one priority. A clean workspace can boost your focus and efficiency, making that math homework a bit more bearable.

Speaking of focus, sticking to short cleaning goals can really change your mindset. It's all about small, manageable steps. Instead of aiming to clean your entire room in one go (which, let's be honest, almost never happens), break it down. Spend five minutes before bed tidying up, or quickly organize your school supplies while waiting for your favorite TV show to start. These tiny efforts fit easily into your schedule and prevent the mess from piling up.

Let's dive deeper into the cleaning calendar. Grab a planner or use an app on your phone. Write down specific cleaning tasks for different days of the week. Keep it realistic—don't overload any single day. This helps make cleaning a routine rather than a panic-induced frenzy before guests arrive. Plus, having a visual reminder keeps you accountable. Check off tasks as you complete them, giving yourself a mini high-five each time. Over time, these proactive habits will become second nature, and you'll wonder how you ever lived without them.

To wrap things up, remember the importance of self-compassion. On those days when everything feels out of control, and your space looks like a tornado hit it, take a deep breath. It's perfectly fine to have off days. Cut yourself some slack and focus on what you've managed to achieve rather than what's left undone. Embrace the messiness as part of your journey. After all, life's too short to stress over a few stray socks or a cluttered desk. By maintaining a flexible, forgiving attitude, you foster resilience and adaptability, making it easier to bounce back and tackle the mess once you have the energy.

By now, you've got a treasure chest of practical tips for keeping your space clean and clutter-free. From making your bed every morning to creating an organized study area, these habits may seem small but pack a big punch in making your life smoother and more enjoyable. Remember, it's not about perfection—no one expects your room to look like it's straight out of a magazine. It's about gradually weaving these routines into your daily life so that tidying up becomes almost second nature.

So, why not start with just one thing? Pick one habit from this chapter and give it a shot for a week. Maybe it's loading the dishwasher after meals or wiping down your bathroom sink each morning. See how it feels and notice the difference it makes. With a bit of consistency and a positive attitude, you'll find yourself on the path to a cleaner, happier living space in no time. And hey, if you miss a day, cut yourself some slack! The most important thing is to keep moving forward, one small step at a time.

CHAPTER 5

BASIC AUTO MAINTENANCE

Basic Auto Maintenance

You're cruising down the highway with your friends on an epic road trip when suddenly, one of your tires gives out. In moments like these, knowing basic car maintenance can save the day. It's not just for the pros—understanding how to check tire pressure and oil levels can save you time, money, and a lot of stress. With a few simple skills, you'll be ready to tackle any roadside challenge with confidence!

In this chapter, we're diving into the essentials of keeping your car in tip-top shape and ready for whatever comes its way. We'll cover how to check and maintain tire pressure so your ride remains smooth and safe. You'll learn step-by-step instructions on using a tire pressure gauge (trust me, it's easier than doing a TikTok dance). Also, don't miss out on tips for when to inflate those tires because, yes, the weather can mess with them. By the end of this chapter, not only will you be equipped with the knowledge to keep your car running efficiently, but you'll also feel like a total boss handling these auto tasks!

Checking Tire Pressure and Inflation

Understanding Tire Pressure

Tire pressure might sound like a boring, technical term, but trust me, it's super important. You know the feeling of trying to ride a bike with half-flat tires? It's hard to pedal, right? The same goes for cars. Maintaining the correct tire pressure is crucial because it affects how your car handles and its fuel efficiency.

Properly inflated tires grip the road better, which means your car responds more accurately when you steer, brake, or accelerate. Under-inflated tires can make handling sluggish and increase stopping distances, making the car less safe to drive. Over-inflated tires can be just as bad, making the ride bumpy and reducing the tire's contact with the road, which can also mess with handling. So yeah, getting the tire pressure right isn't just about avoiding flat tires; it's about keeping your car driving smoothly and safely.

How to Check Tire Pressure

Alright, now let's get into the nitty-gritty of checking your tire pressure. It's not rocket science—promise!

First things first, you'll need a tire pressure gauge. These are pretty cheap and available at most auto stores. There are digital ones and old-school stick types, both work fine.

Find the Right Pressure: Your car's manual or a sticker on the driver's side door jamb will tell you the ideal tire pressure for your vehicle.

Check When Cold: Always check tire pressure when the tires are cold. This doesn't mean freezing cold but before you've driven more than a couple of miles. Driving heats up the tires and can give a false reading.

Remove the Valve Cap: Unscrew the cap from the air valve on the tire.

Place the Gauge: Press the tire pressure gauge onto the valve stem. If you hear a hiss, adjust the angle to ensure you're getting a proper seal.

Read the Gauge: Look at the reading on your gauge. Compare this number to your car's recommended tire pressure.

Adjust if Necessary: If the pressure is too low, add air until you reach the recommended level. If it's too high, press the valve lightly to let out some air.

When to Inflate Tires

So, you've checked your tire pressure and found out it's off. Now what? Here's when and how you should inflate them.

Firstly, get in the habit of checking your tire pressure at least once a month and before any long trips. Seasonal changes can affect tire pressure more than you'd think. Cold weather usually lowers tire pressure while hot weather can cause it to rise. Both extremes aren't good for your tires or your safety.

In winter, you might find yourself needing to top off the air in your tires more frequently. In summer, you may need to bleed off excess air. Always adjust to the manufacturer's recommendation found in your owner's manual or the sticker mentioned earlier.

When you do need to inflate your tires, most gas stations have an air pump. Just park so the hose reaches all four tires, set the desired pressure on the machine if it has that option, and fill away. Make sure to recheck the pressure after inflating each tire to avoid overdoing it.

Risks of Improper Tire Maintenance

Okay, let's talk about what happens when you neglect your tires. It's not just about having a flat tire on your hands—though that's a real pain, especially if it happens on the way to something important.

Firstly, poor tire pressure can lead to reduced fuel efficiency. Under-inflated tires create more rolling resistance (think friction), which means your engine has to work harder to keep the car moving. This extra effort burns more fuel, meaning frequent trips to the gas station.

Secondly, improper tire care increases the risk of accidents. Tires in bad shape are more prone to blowouts—especially at higher speeds—which can cause you to lose control of the vehicle. Not fun. Also, as we touched on earlier, incorrect tire pressure can lead to poor handling, making it tough to steer or stop quickly in emergencies.

Lastly, under- or over-inflated tires wear unevenly and more quickly. This ends up being more expensive for you in the long run because you'll need to replace them sooner than expected.

How to Read the Dashboard Warning Lights

Interpreting dashboard warning lights might seem like a daunting task, but once you familiarize yourself with these signals, you'll find they are truly your car's way of communicating with you. Let's start with an overview of common dashboard symbols and their meanings.

First up is the **check engine light.** This little symbol can indicate a variety of issues, ranging from a loose gas cap to something more serious like an engine misfire. The symbol looks like, well, an engine! If this light comes on, your car's computer has detected an issue, and it's important to address it promptly. It may not always be an emergency, but ignoring it could lead to bigger problems down the line.

Another key symbol is the **oil pressure warning light.** This one looks like an old-fashioned oil can. When this light illuminates, it means there's probably an issue with the oil pressure in your engine. This could be due to low oil levels or a problem with the oil pump. It's crucial not to ignore this warning because proper oil pressure is vital for keeping your engine lubricated and running smoothly.

The **battery charge warning light,** coming next, usually appears as a battery icon. If this light turns on while you're driving, it indicates that the battery isn't being charged properly, which could be due to a problem with the alternator, battery, or wiring. You should get this checked out as soon as possible because if the battery dies, your car will too.

Now, let's talk about the **tire pressure monitoring system (TPMS) light.** This symbol looks like an exclamation point inside a horseshoe. When this light comes on, it means one or more of your tires has low pressure. Driving with under-inflated tires can affect your car's handling and fuel efficiency, so it's best to pull over and check the tire pressures right away.

One of the most alarming lights you might see is the **brake warning light.** This could either look like an exclamation mark inside a circle or simply say "BRAKE." If this light comes on, it usually means there's an issue with your braking system. It could be low brake fluid, worn brake pads, or something more serious. Brakes are obviously critical for safety, so don't delay in addressing this warning.

Understanding what these lights mean is just the beginning. Knowing how to react when they illuminate is equally important. Take a look at the list below to see what to do if a warning light comes on.

Check Engine Light:
o Flashing Light: Stop driving immediately. A flashing check engine light indicates a serious issue, like an engine misfire. Pull over safely and turn off the engine to prevent further damage.
o Solid Light: You can usually drive home or to a repair shop. However, don't delay in getting it checked out.

Oil Pressure Warning Light:
o If this light comes on, stop the car immediately and turn off the engine.
o Check the oil level and add oil if needed. If the light stays on, do not continue driving—call for roadside assistance to avoid severe engine damage.

Battery Charge Warning Light:
o Turn off non-essential electrical devices, such as the radio or air conditioning, to reduce the load on the battery.
o Drive straight to a mechanic to have the issue diagnosed before the battery drains completely.

TPMS (Tire Pressure Monitoring System) Light:
o Carry a portable tire inflator in your car for situations like this.
o When the light comes on, find a safe place to stop and check the tire pressures.
o Inflate any tires that are low to the recommended pressure listed in your car's manual or on the door jamb sticker.

Brake Warning Light:
o First, ensure that the parking brake isn't engaged. Release it if it is.
o If the parking brake isn't the issue, check the brake fluid level.
o Low brake fluid can indicate worn brake pads or a leak. Get your car inspected by a professional immediately.

These directions will help you know what to do when dashboard warning lights appear, ensuring you can handle minor car issues safely and efficiently.

Keeping a reference guide handy, whether it's your car's manual or a dedicated app, fosters independence in troubleshooting these issues. There are several apps available that list all possible dashboard symbols and their meanings. These tools can be lifesavers, especially if you're unsure about a particular warning light. Car manuals also often include troubleshooting tips and step-by-step guides for basic maintenance tasks.

Lastly, connecting warning lights with routine maintenance can help in early detection of potential issues. Regular oil changes, battery checks, and tire pressure monitoring can prevent many of these warning lights from appearing in the first place. Think of routine maintenance as a way to keep the conversation with your car positive and avoid those stress-inducing dashboard alerts.

Replacing Windshield Wiper Blades

Alright, let's get to the nitty-gritty of replacing windshield wiper blades! First up, you may wonder how you even know when it's time for new wiper blades. Imagine you're driving on a rainy day, and instead of a clear window, your wipers leave streaks as they swoosh back and forth. Or even worse, they start skipping parts of your windshield entirely. These are clear signs that your wiper blades are calling it quits.

Now that we've established when it's time for a change, let's talk about how to choose the right wiper blades for your car. Not all wiper blades are made equal, and not every blade will fit your vehicle. The best place to start? Check your car's owner manual for the size specifications. You can also find this information online by searching for wiper blade sizes specific to your car's make and model. When you're at the store, look for wiper blades that mention compatibility with your vehicle. Some brands even have handy guides to make sure you grab the right pair.

Okay, now we're armed with the knowledge of when and what to buy. Let's dive into the step-by-step guide on replacing those old, sad wiper blades. Don't worry; it sounds scarier than it is!

1. Lift the Wiper Arm: Start by gently lifting the wiper arm away from the windshield. It should stand upright on its own, but be careful—it's spring-loaded, and you don't want it snapping back.

2. Remove the Old Blade: Look for a small tab underneath the wiper blade where it connects to the wiper arm. Press this tab and slide the blade downwards off the hook. If your blades use a different type of attachment, check the instructions on your new wiper blades—they often come with pictures!

3. Attach the New Blade: Take your new wiper blade and slide it onto the wiper arm. You'll usually hear a click when it's securely in place. Give it a gentle tug to make sure it's locked.

4. Lower the Wiper Arm: Carefully lower the wiper arm back onto the windshield. Make sure they rest properly and test them out by turning on your wipers.

Voila! You've just replaced your wiper blades. Celebrate with a happy dance, because you're officially a DIY car maintenance pro.

But wait, there's more! To make your new wiper blades last longer, here are some care tips that'll keep them in top shape. First, keep your windshield clean. Dirt and grime can wear out your wiper blades faster, so give your windshield a good cleaning whenever you fill up on gas. Regularly inspecting and cleaning your wiper blades with a damp cloth can also prevent debris from scratching your windshield.

Another tip is to protect your wiper blades from extreme weather. In winter, try to lift your wiper arms off the windshield if you know it's going to snow. This way, they won't freeze to the glass. During summer, park your car in the shade to prevent the rubber on the blades from becoming brittle due to heat exposure.

And there you have it! A comprehensive guide on identifying when to replace, choosing the right wiper blades, installing them, and ensuring they last long. Car maintenance doesn't have to be daunting. With these simple steps, you've got one less thing to worry about on the road.

What to Have in a Basic Car Emergency Kit

When it comes to driving, you never know when life might throw a curveball your way. Being prepared for unexpected situations can make a world of difference. So, let's talk about putting together that essential car emergency kit. It's like having a little guardian angel in your trunk, ready to help out when things get dicey on the road.

First up, let's break down the must-have items for your emergency kit. This isn't just some hodgepodge of random stuff; each item plays a vital role in keeping you safe and prepared. At the top of the list is a first aid kit. You'd be surprised how often a Band-Aid or some antiseptic wipes come in handy. Next, grab a flashlight with extra batteries. Trust me, if you're ever stuck in the dark, this will be your new best friend. Jumper cables are another lifesaver. If your battery dies, these bad boys can help get you back on the road with a quick jump from a friendly passerby.

Other essentials? Think about carrying a multi-tool with features like pliers, screwdrivers, and knives – it's a compact and versatile hero. Don't forget a tire pressure gauge and a can of tire sealant – crucial for those unexpected flat tires. A set of basic tools, including wrenches and a jack, is also a good idea. And hey, toss in some non-perishable snacks and bottled water. If you're stranded for a while, you'll thank yourself for thinking ahead.

Now let's get into the nitty-gritty of creating a personalized emergency kit. Start by assessing your driving habits. Do you take long road trips, or mostly stick to city driving? Are you in an area prone to severe weather, like snowstorms or heavy rains? Tailoring your kit to your specific needs will ensure you're covered no matter what.

Begin by gathering all the aforementioned essentials. Lay them out and see what you've got. Then think about your regular routes and add any extras you might need. For instance, if you drive in snowy conditions, add some instant hand warmers, thermal blankets, and maybe even some kitty litter for traction if you get stuck in the snow. If you're more of a desert driver, consider extra water and sunblock.

Once you have everything, find a sturdy container to keep it all organized. You want something durable, easy to carry, and preferably waterproof. Make sure it's easily accessible in your trunk, not buried under a pile of sports gear and shopping bags. Over time, make it a habit to update your kit. Check expiration dates on items like food, water, and medical supplies every few months. Replace batteries regularly so they don't run out when you need them most.

Alright, moving on to some safety considerations during emergencies. When trouble strikes, your first move should be getting to safety. Pull over to the side of the road, ideally far enough away from traffic. Turn on your hazard lights to alert other drivers that something's up. They're like your car's way of waving a red flag, saying "Hey, pay attention!"

If it's a more serious situation, like an accident or breakdown in a dangerous spot, don't hesitate to call emergency services. It's always better to be safe than sorry. Stay inside your vehicle if there's heavy traffic around you. Your car provides a layer of protection against other vehicles.

Understand the basics of using each item in your kit. If you need to jump-start your car, make sure you know how to connect the jumper cables properly. Red clamp to positive terminal, black clamp to negative – pretty straightforward, but essential knowledge. Browse through the instructions on your tire sealant and have a practice run on how to change a tire with your jack and tools, just in case.

Lastly, let's talk about tailoring your kits for different driving scenarios. Not all emergencies look the same, and neither should your preparedness strategy. If you're gearing up for winter, pack extra blankets, warm clothing, an ice scraper, and maybe even a small shovel. Breaking down in freezing conditions without these items could turn a minor inconvenience into a major headache.

For long-distance travelers, think bigger. Add a portable phone charger, a camping stove with fuel, and a reflective vest. These items aren't just for comfort; they can be critical if you're stuck in a remote area without cell service for extended periods.

Urban commuters might focus more on immediate necessities. Compact items like a whistle, spare cash, and a detailed roadmap (yes, a physical one) could prove invaluable. Imagine your phone dying and GPS not working – having a map and knowing where you're headed suddenly becomes a game-changer.

In this chapter, we dove into the basics of car care and emergency preparedness, giving you the lowdown on keeping your wheels safe and sound. From checking tire pressure to understanding those pesky dashboard warning lights, you've now got the skills to spot issues before they become major headaches. Remember, knowing how to replace windshield wiper blades or pack a solid emergency kit can make all the difference when you're out on the road.

Whether it's avoiding a flat tire drama or feeling like a pro when those dashboard lights flash, you're now equipped with some essential car know-how. Keep practicing these handy tips and tricks, and soon enough, you'll be the go-to car guru among your friends. Stay safe, keep learning, and always trust in your newfound car-savvy confidence!

CHAPTER 6

HOME DIY PROJECTS

Home DIY Projects

Getting into home DIY projects is like unlocking a secret world where you can make your living space truly your own. Instead of relying on someone else to fix things or add those little personal touches, you'll be the one making the magic happen. It's all about discovering that fabulous sense of accomplishment when you've nailed (sometimes literally) a project and made something better with your own two hands. This chapter is your gateway to becoming that handy individual who isn't fazed by minor household issues but rather sees them as opportunities to get crafty and creative.

In this chapter, we'll dive straight into the basics, starting with mastering essential tools like hammers and screwdrivers. You'll learn the ins and outs of how to use them safely and effectively, transforming from a newbie into a confident DIYer in no time. We'll walk you through fun and manageable first-time projects that won't just help you practice your newfound skills but also jazz up your space instantly. From hanging picture frames perfectly to fixing that annoyingly loose cabinet door, you'll gain practical know-how that will make you feel capable and self-sufficient. So, grab your toolkit, and let's start turning those Pinterest dreams into reality!

Using a hammer and screwdriver effectively

Understanding how to use essential tools is a great way to start feeling more confident and independent in managing your living space. This section will introduce you to some basic hand tools—hammers and screwdrivers—and walk you through their uses, safety precautions, and simple practice tasks to get you started.

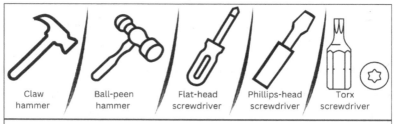

| Claw hammer | Ball-peen hammer | Flat-head screwdriver | Phillips-head screwdriver | Torx screwdriver |

First things first, there are several types of hammers and screwdrivers, each designed for specific tasks. For instance, a **claw hammer** is the most common type you'll find at home. It has a dual-purpose head: one side is flat for hammering nails, while the other side, known as the claw, is used for removing them. A **ball-peen hammer**, on the other hand, has a rounded head and is generally used in metalworking. Understanding these differences can help you choose the right tool for the job.

Screwdrivers come in a variety of shapes and sizes too. The two most common types are the **flat-head (or slotted) screwdriver** and the **Phillips-head screwdriver**. The flat-head is used for screws with a linear slot, while the Phillips-head is designed for screws with a cross shape. There are also **Torx screwdrivers** with star-shaped tips, often found in electronics or automotive work. Knowing which screwdriver to use will make any task easier and prevent damage to both the tool and the screw.

Now that you're familiar with the types of hammers and screwdrivers, let's move on to how to use them effectively. When nailing, hold the nail near its point to steady it. Strike lightly at first to drive the nail in without bending it, then apply heavier blows as it becomes stable. Make sure to keep your fingers away from the nail's path. This reduces your risk of injury and helps you hammer more efficiently.

For screwing, always match the screwdriver to the screw type. Place the screwdriver tip into the screw head and turn it clockwise to tighten. Use steady pressure to avoid stripping the screw head. If the screw seems stuck, don't force it—this could strip the head or break the screw. Instead, try applying a little bit of lubricant or switching to a more suitable screwdriver.

Safety should always be your top priority. Always wear eye protection when using hand tools to shield your eyes from flying debris. Gloves can protect your hands, but make sure they are snug so you can still grip the tools properly. Being aware of your surroundings and ensuring good lighting can also prevent accidents. Don't forget to keep your tools in good condition; clean them after each use and store them properly to prolong their lifespan (True Value, 2020).

Taking safety seriously also means knowing your limits. If a tool seems damaged or you're unsure how to use it, don't hesitate to ask for help. Never carry pointed tools like screwdrivers in your pockets, and always handle sharp edges with care (Corporation, 2015). These small steps can go a long way in preventing injuries.

Once you've got the basics down, it's time for some simple practice projects. One great starter project is hanging a picture frame. To do this, you'll need a hammer, nails or screws, a measuring tape, and a level. First, decide where you want to hang the frame and measure the distance from the floor to ensure it's at the right height. Mark the spot lightly with a pencil. Next, hold the frame up to the spot and use the level to make sure it's straight. You can place a small piece of painter's tape on the wall to mark the points where you'll insert the nails or screws.

When you're ready to start, gently tap the nails or screw in the screws at the marked spots, making sure they're secure but not over-tightened. Finally, hang the frame and check once more with the level to ensure it's straight. This simple task will help you become more comfortable with using a hammer and screwdriver and give you a sense of accomplishment.

Another easy project is fixing loose cabinet doors. Often, this requires just a few turns of a screwdriver. Open the cabinet door and locate the screws holding the hinge in place. Tighten them until the door swings smoothly but remains sturdy. It's a small fix that makes a significant difference in your everyday life, and it reinforces your new skills.

These initial projects might seem minor, but they're a great way to build your confidence and familiarize yourself with your tools. Each successful task will make you more independent and capable of handling more complex home maintenance in the future.

As you continue learning and practicing, remember that everyone starts as a beginner. Mistakes are simply part of the learning process. The key is to stay curious and never be afraid to ask questions or seek additional resources. With each project, you'll gain valuable experience and become more adept at maintaining and personalizing your living space.

Steps to fixing a leaky faucet

Let's dive into the world of home DIY projects, focusing on one of the most common issues: a leaky faucet. This guide is all about giving you practical steps to handle this household problem confidently and efficiently. Whether you're dealing with a dripping tap in the bathroom or kitchen, we've got you covered.

Identifying Different Faucet Types

First things first, you need to know what type of faucet you're dealing with. There are four main types:

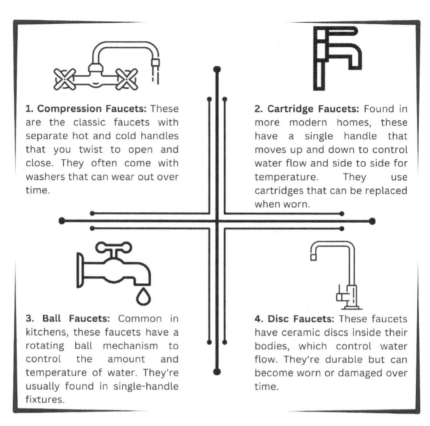

1. **Compression Faucets:** These are the classic faucets with separate hot and cold handles that you twist to open and close. They often come with washers that can wear out over time.

2. **Cartridge Faucets:** Found in more modern homes, these have a single handle that moves up and down to control water flow and side to side for temperature. They use cartridges that can be replaced when worn.

3. **Ball Faucets:** Common in kitchens, these faucets have a rotating ball mechanism to control the amount and temperature of water. They're usually found in single-handle fixtures.

4. **Disc Faucets:** These faucets have ceramic discs inside their bodies, which control water flow. They're durable but can become worn or damaged over time.

Knowing your faucet type will help streamline the repair process and ensure you have the right tools and materials on hand.

Comprehensive Tool and Materials Checklist

Before jumping into the repair, gather these essential tools and materials:

- Adjustable wrench
- Phillips and flathead screwdrivers
- Replacement O-rings or washers (specific to your faucet type)
- Plumber's tape
- Plumber's grease
- Spare parts like a new cartridge if needed
- Protective cloth or rag
- Small bowl (to hold screws and small parts)

Having everything ready before you start will make the whole process smoother. Plus, it saves you from having to stop mid-repair to hunt for a missing tool.

Step-by-Step Repair Instructions

Now, let's get to the nitty-gritty of fixing that leaky faucet.

1. Turn Off the Water Supply

Locate the shut-off valves under the sink and turn them clockwise to stop the water flow. Open the faucet to drain any remaining water. This step is crucial to avoid any unnecessary mess.

2. Disassemble the Faucet

Use your screwdriver to remove the handle. For compression faucets, you'll need to unscrew the valve stem to access the washer. For ball, cartridge, and disc faucets, remove the handle and any retaining nuts to expose the internal parts. Keep track of each component; it's helpful to lay them out in the order you remove them.

3. Diagnose the Problem

Look closely at the internal components. Common issues include worn-out washers, O-rings, corroded valve seats, or damaged cartridges. Even small imperfections can cause leaks, so inspect each part carefully.

4. Replace Faulty Parts

Swap out any worn or damaged parts with new ones. Make sure replacement washers and O-rings are the correct size and shape for your faucet. Apply plumber's grease to O-rings and washers if recommended. If you have a cartridge or disc faucet, replace the entire cartridge if necessary.

5. Reassemble the Faucet

Put your faucet back together in reverse order of how you disassembled it. Ensure everything is tight but don't over-tighten, as this can damage the parts. Use plumber's tape on threaded connections to prevent leaks.

6. Turn On the Water Supply

Turn the shut-off valves counterclockwise to restore the water flow. Open the faucet to check for leaks and ensure everything is working properly.

Tips on Testing Repairs and Preventing Future Leaks

After reassembling the faucet, run some water through it and watch closely for any leaks. Tighten connections slightly if you notice any drips, but be cautious not to overtighten.

Here are some tips to ensure long-lasting repairs and prevent future leaks:

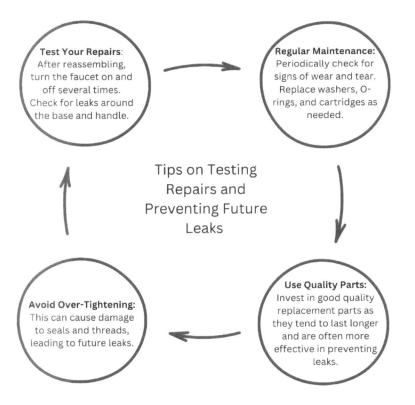

Test Your Repairs: After reassembling, turn the faucet on and off several times. Check for leaks around the base and handle.

Regular Maintenance: Periodically check for signs of wear and tear. Replace washers, O-rings, and cartridges as needed.

Tips on Testing Repairs and Preventing Future Leaks

Avoid Over-Tightening: This can cause damage to seals and threads, leading to future leaks.

Use Quality Parts: Invest in good quality replacement parts as they tend to last longer and are often more effective in preventing leaks.

Creating personalized decor items

Encouraging creativity and self-expression through DIY decor projects can be an incredibly rewarding experience for you! By making your own unique, homemade items, you not only enhance your living spaces but also boost your confidence and emotional well-being. Let's dive into some fantastic ideas and guidelines to help you get started.

First up is the overview of material choices. When embarking on a DIY decor project, it's essential to consider recycled and sustainable options. Not only are these materials better for the environment, but they often come with a creative twist that can make your projects truly stand out. Think about using old newspapers, magazines, or even cardboard boxes. These items can be transformed into beautiful pieces of art with just a bit of imagination. Additionally, look around your home for objects that might otherwise be discarded—like glass jars, fabric scraps, or old buttons. These can all be repurposed into stunning decorative elements that reflect your personal style.

Next, let's move on to step-by-step guidance for crafting specific decor items like photo frames or wall art. One simple project to try is creating a custom photo frame. Start by gathering your materials: an old cardboard box, scissors, glue, paint, and any embellishments you have on hand (think stickers, beads, or ribbon). Cut out a rectangular piece from the cardboard as the base of your frame and another smaller rectangle within it to hold your picture. Paint the base in your favorite color and once it's dry, glue on your chosen embellishments. Slide a photo behind the inner cutout, and voilà—you've got a personalized photo frame ready to display!

For wall art, consider making a collage using old magazines and newspapers. Begin by selecting a theme, such as nature or fashion. Cut out relevant images and arrange them on a large piece of cardboard or canvas in a layout that pleases you. Once you're happy with the arrangement, glue the images down. To add a magical touch, sprinkle some glitter or outline certain sections with markers. This kind of project allows you to express yourself freely while creating a statement piece for your wall.

Adding personal touches to your creations is what will make them truly unique and meaningful. Consider incorporating elements that are significant to you, such as photos with friends, tickets from events, or small souvenirs from trips. These additions turn your DIY projects into visual stories of your life. For example, if you're working on a corkboard, pin up some of your favorite polaroids, concert tickets, and mementos to give it a personalized flair. Not only does this make your space feel more like you, but every glance at the board will evoke happy memories and feelings of pride in your work.

Displaying your homemade decor and sharing it with friends and family is the final step. There are endless ways to showcase your creations, depending on the item. Photo frames can be placed on bedside tables or hung on walls in a gallery-style arrangement. Wall art can take center stage above your bed or couch, becoming a vibrant focal point in the room. If you've made smaller items like decorated jars or trinket boxes, consider placing them on shelves where they can be admired and easily accessed.

Don't forget to share your masterpieces with friends and family! Hosting a craft night where everyone gets to make their own decor item can be a fun way to bond and inspire each other. You could even start a mini craft club, where you meet regularly to work on new projects together. It's a great way to foster a supportive community and exchange creative ideas.

Unclogging a bathroom or kitchen drain

When it comes to managing common household problems, one of the biggest challenges you'll face is dealing with clogged drains. Clogs can be more than just an inconvenience; they can cause significant damage if not addressed promptly. But don't worry! With a few essential skills and tools, you can handle most clogs yourself, fostering both independence and self-sufficiency.

First things first, let's tackle what causes those pesky clogs in the first place. Understanding the common causes can help you prevent them from happening. Food waste, hair, grease, oil, soap scum, and foreign objects are frequent culprits. For example, have you ever noticed your kitchen sink clogging up after washing dishes? That's because food particles and grease love to stick around and build up over time. In the bathroom, hair and soap scum are classic offenders that often lead to slow drains or total blockages.

Now that we know what causes clogs, let's talk about prevention. The simplest way to avoid a clogged drain is to be mindful of what goes down it. Avoid pouring grease, oils, or fatty substances into the sink. Instead, let them cool and dispose of them in the trash. Use drain guards or screens to catch hair, food particles, and other debris. And remember, only flush toilet paper and human waste down the toilet—everything else belongs in the trash.

But sometimes, despite our best efforts, clogs happen. When they do, having the right tools can make all the difference. Here are some essential tools you'll need:

1. A Plunger: This handy tool uses suction to dislodge clogs. It's simple yet effective for minor clogs.

2. Drain Snake: Also known as a plumber's snake, this long, flexible tool can reach deep into pipes to break up clogs.

3. Baking Soda and Vinegar: These natural solutions work wonders for breaking down organic material in the pipes.

4. Chemical Drain Cleaners: While less eco-friendly, these can be useful for stubborn clogs when used sparingly.

Alright, let's dive into the nitty-gritty of unclogging a drain. Here's a step-by-step guide:

Step 1: Assess the Situation Before diving in, take a moment to assess how severe the clog is. If water is draining slowly, it's likely a minor issue. But if there's standing water that won't budge, you might have a bigger problem on your hands.

Step 2: Use Boiling Water For minor clogs, try pouring boiling hot water down the drain. Do this slowly and intermittently to give the heat time to break up the clog. Be careful not to burn yourself!

Step 3: Plunging Technique If boiling water doesn't work, grab your plunger. Place the plunger over the drain and ensure there's enough water to cover the rubber cup. Push down gently at first to force out air, then plunge vigorously in short, quick motions. The suction should help dislodge the clog. Repeat this process several times if needed.

Step 4: Baking Soda and Vinegar Still clogged? Pour half a cup of baking soda down the drain, followed by half a cup of vinegar. Let it sit for about 30 minutes. This mixture creates a chemical reaction that can help break down organic material. Afterward, flush the drain with hot water.

Step 5: Drain Snake Savvy If the clog persists, it's time to bring out the big guns—the drain snake. Insert the snake into the drain and turn the handle clockwise to maneuver it through the pipes. When you feel resistance, you've hit the clog. Rotate the snake to break it apart or pull it back to remove the debris. Run water to check if the clog is cleared.

Step 6: Chemical Solutions As a last resort, consider using a chemical drain cleaner. Follow the instructions carefully, as these chemicals can be harsh and dangerous if misused. Wear gloves and ensure proper ventilation in the area. Pour the cleaner down the drain and let it sit for the recommended time before flushing with water.

When to Call a Professional Sometimes, no matter how hard you try, the clog just won't budge. Knowing when to call a

LIFE SKILLS PLAYBOOK FOR TEEN GIRLS

professional can save you a lot of stress and potential damage. If you've tried all the above methods without success, it might be time to seek expert help. Persistent clogs could indicate more serious issues deep within the plumbing system that requires specialized equipment and expertise.

In conclusion, managing household clogs doesn't have to be daunting. By understanding the common causes and taking preventative measures, you can avoid many clog-related headaches. Equip yourself with essential tools and follow these clear steps to tackle clogs efficiently. And remember, calling a professional isn't a sign of defeat—sometimes it's the smartest move for maintaining a smoothly functioning home.

Now that you've got the basics down, it's time to dive into some fun and rewarding projects. From hanging picture frames to fixing cabinet doors, these small tasks will boost your confidence and make your space uniquely yours. Don't worry about making mistakes— they're all part of the learning curve. Stay curious, keep practicing, and soon you'll be tackling even bigger DIY challenges with ease. Happy hammering!

CHAPTER 7

FINANCIAL LITERACY

Financial Literacy

Ever feel like managing money is a mystery? It doesn't have to be! Learning the basics of financial literacy is all about gaining the skills to handle your cash flow and make smart decisions that lead to greater independence. After all, who doesn't want to feel like they've got life under control? This chapter breaks down everything you need to know into simple, easy steps, making navigating your finances not just manageable, but surprisingly fun!

You'll start by getting to grips with creating and sticking to a budget, an essential skill that can turn chaos into order. From understanding where your money comes from and goes, to setting achievable financial goals, we've got you covered. Then, you'll delve into savings accounts and the wonders of compound interest—learning how to make your money grow while barely lifting a finger.

We'll also explore the ins and outs of using debit cards responsibly and wrap up with smart shopping strategies to keep those impulse buys in check. So buckle up; you're about to become financially savvy without breaking a sweat!

Creating and Sticking to a Budget

Budgeting is like having a BFF who's got your financial back. It helps you manage your money so you can splurge on that cute top or save up for an epic summer trip with the besties. Let's dive into how budgeting can make your financial life easier and more fun!

First things first, understanding income and expenses is super important. Think of it as knowing where your allowance, part-time job paycheck, or birthday money is coming from and where it's going. This knowledge helps you avoid those dreaded moments when you're left wondering where all your money went. Say you get $50 a week from various sources; keeping track means you'll know if you can afford to go out for pizza and still have enough for that new phone case you've been eyeing. Without this info, overspending becomes way too easy, and nobody wants to be stuck at home because they're broke.

Now, setting realistic goals is key. Imagine wanting to save for a car but also loving to shop. Prioritizing needs over wants means deciding what's more important in the long run. For example, instead of buying a new outfit every week, consider putting some cash aside each month for your car fund. A guideline here: List out your needs (like saving for college or a car) and your wants (like extra accessories or dining out). Allocate your money wisely, ensuring your savings goals are met while still allowing room for fun stuff. This balance helps you meet short-term goals, like buying a concert ticket, and long-term ones, like paying for college, without feeling deprived.

Using budgeting tools can make this whole process so much easier. There are awesome apps designed to help you keep track of your spending without pulling your hair out. Apps like Mint or YNAB (You Need A Budget) can categorize your expenses, send you reminders, and even alert you when you're about to overspend. You could also use a simple spreadsheet if you're more into DIY budgeting. The point is, these tools turn budgeting from a boring task into something engaging and interactive. Plus, seeing your progress can be super motivating! Set reminders in these apps to review your budget weekly, making adjustments as needed to stay on track.

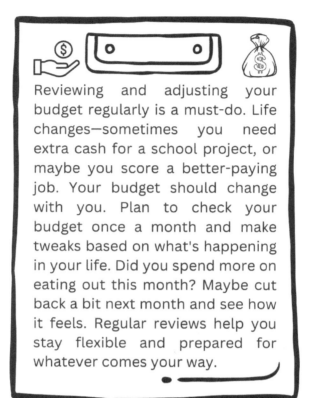

Reviewing and adjusting your budget regularly is a must-do. Life changes—sometimes you need extra cash for a school project, or maybe you score a better-paying job. Your budget should change with you. Plan to check your budget once a month and make tweaks based on what's happening in your life. Did you spend more on eating out this month? Maybe cut back a bit next month and see how it feels. Regular reviews help you stay flexible and prepared for whatever comes your way.

Understanding Savings Accounts and Interest

Alright, let's talk about the essentials of savings and the nitty-gritty of how interest works. It's super important to have a good grasp on these concepts to keep your finances in top shape.

The Basics of Savings Accounts

First off, let's dive into savings accounts. Think of them as your financial safe haven—a place where you stash away money that you're not going to touch for daily expenses. It's like having two drawers: one for spending money and another for keeping money safe for future needs. By separating everyday spending from savings, you avoid dipping into funds meant for bigger goals or emergencies. Plus, savings accounts often come with better security measures to prevent unauthorized access.

The Power of Compound Interest

Now, onto compound interest, which is basically the magic ingredient in the recipe for growing your savings. Compound interest means you earn interest not just on your initial deposit (the principal) but also on any interest the account has already accumulated. So, your money starts to snowball over time. For example, if you put $100 into a savings account with 5% annual interest, you'd have $105 at the end of the year. But here's the kicker—the next year, you earn interest on $105, not just the original $100, so you'd end up with $110.25. Starting early gives this snowball plenty of time to grow huge. Every bit counts, and starting to save even a small amount now can make a big difference later on (Kopp, 2021).

Choosing the Right Savings Account

Picking the right savings account is like finding the perfect pair of jeans—there are a lot out there, but not every fit is right for everyone. When choosing a savings account, consider factors like fees, interest rates, and how easily you can access your money. Some accounts have high fees that can eat into your savings, while others have better interest rates that help your money grow faster. Accessibility is key too. If you'll need to withdraw money occasionally, look for an account without hefty withdrawal penalties. Make sure your account is insured by the Federal Deposit Insurance Corporation (FDIC), meaning your deposits are protected up to

$250,000 if the bank fails. Shop around and compare before committing ("How Interest Works on a Savings Account," n.d.).

Setting Savings Goals

Finally, setting savings goals is crucial. Think about what you're saving for—a new phone, college, a car, or even travel. By having specific targets, it's easier to stay motivated. Say you want a new laptop that costs $1,200; break it down into smaller, manageable goals. Maybe save $100 each month for a year, and you'll hit your target without feeling overwhelmed. Keep track of your progress, and celebrate small victories to keep yourself motivated. This approach helps build consistent saving habits over time.

Putting It All Together

Mixing all these ingredients together—basic knowledge of savings accounts, understanding compound interest, choosing the right account, and setting clear goals—is the recipe for financial success. Each element complements the other, creating a solid foundation for managing your money wisely. As you get comfortable navigating these waters, you'll find it becomes second nature, and your bank balance will thank you for it.

Understanding these aspects now sets you up for smarter financial decisions down the road. Remember, financial literacy isn't just about knowing terms and definitions; it's about applying what you know to make sound decisions that benefit you in the long run. So start today, whether it's opening a savings account, learning about interest, or setting your savings goal. Your future self will be grateful for the actions you take now.

Don't wait until later to start saving. The sooner you begin, the more time you give your money to grow through the power of compound interest. Every dollar saved today can turn into significant amounts over time, especially when you understand and utilize the strategies discussed here.

Using Debit Cards Responsibly

Understanding Debit vs. Credit

Alright, let's kick things off with understanding the difference between debit and credit cards. It's like comparing apples and oranges—both tasty but totally different! When you use a debit card, you're spending money straight from your bank account. Picture this: every time you swipe that card, it's like plucking cash out of your wallet. This is super handy because it means you won't end up owing money later.

On the other hand, a credit card is more like borrowing money. When you use it, you're saying, "Hey bank, spot me this amount for now, and I'll pay you back later." The catch here is that if you don't pay it back in time, you'll owe extra money on top of what you borrowed. So, while a credit card can build credit history and offer perks, it requires a lot more discipline to avoid ending up in debt. Knowing these differences can help you choose wisely which card to pull out of your wallet!

Managing Debit Card Transactions

Now, let's chat about managing those debit card transactions. Think of your bank account as a garden. If you don't water it regularly (in this case, keep an eye on it), things could start wilting. One of the best ways to stay on top of your finances is by checking your account balance regularly. Luckily, there are banking apps that let you do this in real-time, turning your smartphone into a mini financial toolkit.

Using these apps makes it easy to see how much you've spent and how much is left in your account. It's like having a personal assistant who keeps track of your money. No more surprises at the checkout counter! Also, enabling transaction alerts can give you instant notifications whenever your card is used, so you're always in the loop. Banking apps can also categorize your spending, helping you see where your money is going—whether it's shopping, food, or entertainment. Regular checks and keeping tabs on your spending habits will make sure you don't run into any unexpected overdrafts.

Handling Lost or Stolen Cards

Oops! We've all been there—losing a card or finding out it's been stolen. The good news is, handling it effectively can save you a lot of stress. The first thing you should do is report it immediately. Don't wait around hoping it will magically turn up in your laundry basket. Contact your bank as soon as you notice it's missing. They can freeze the card to prevent anyone else from using it.

Besides reporting it lost or stolen, it's a smart move to regularly review your transactions. This way, even if someone sneaky got hold of your details, you can catch unauthorized activities quickly. And remember, the sooner you report it, the better protected you'll be against fraud. Some banks might even allow you to freeze and unfreeze your card through their app—an easy way to add an extra layer of security.

In cases where your debit card is stolen and used, consider filing a police report. It might sound a little extreme, but keeping a copy of the police report can provide extra support when dealing with your bank to get reimbursed for any fraudulent charges. (Lerner, n.d.)

Using ATMs Safely

Okay, let's talk about using ATMs safely. Think of an ATM as a vending machine for cash—but one that requires a bit of caution. First off, always choose well-lit and busy locations. Dark alleyway ATMs might feel like scenes from a horror movie for a reason—they aren't safe! Stick to ATMs inside banks or well-trafficked areas to ensure your safety.

While at the ATM, be aware of your surroundings. Make sure no one is hovering too close or trying to peek over your shoulder. Shield your PIN entry with your hand, like a magician hiding their secrets. And if something feels off, trust your gut and find another ATM.

Also, you might want to watch out for those unnecessary fees. Sometimes, using an out-of-network ATM can lead to extra charges. It's like buying a candy bar and paying double just for the convenience! To avoid this, stick to ATMs affiliated with your bank whenever possible.

And if your banking app supports it, consider using cardless ATM access. This lets you withdraw cash using a temporary code from your app, adding an extra layer of security since there's no card to steal.

Smart Shopping Strategies to Avoid Impulse Buying

One of the most effective ways to prevent impulsive spending is by making a shopping list. Think about it: how often have you walked into a store with the intention of buying just one item, only to leave with a cart full of stuff you didn't plan to get? Creating a shopping list can help you avoid these temptations. It provides a clear plan for your purchases, which makes it easier to stick to your budget and focus on what you truly need rather than what catches your eye in the moment.

To make this work, jot down everything you need before heading out. This might include groceries, school supplies, or even that cute new outfit you've been eyeing—just as long as it's already on the list. Apps like Google Keep or AnyList can be super helpful for organizing your lists and even sharing them with friends or family members. By sticking to your pre-planned items, you're less likely to toss those unnecessary extras into your cart.

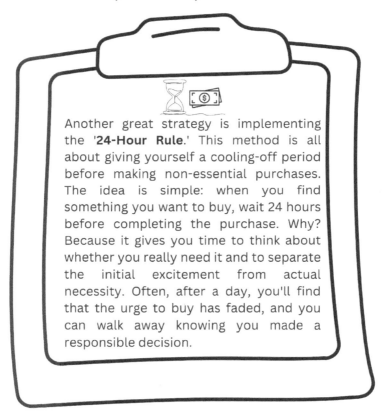

Another great strategy is implementing the **'24-Hour Rule**.' This method is all about giving yourself a cooling-off period before making non-essential purchases. The idea is simple: when you find something you want to buy, wait 24 hours before completing the purchase. Why? Because it gives you time to think about whether you really need it and to separate the initial excitement from actual necessity. Often, after a day, you'll find that the urge to buy has faded, and you can walk away knowing you made a responsible decision.

During these 24 hours, take the time to do some research. Read reviews, compare prices, and consider whether the purchase aligns with your needs and budget. This pause not only helps prevent impulsive buying but also ensures that when you do decide to spend, you're getting the best value for your money. For instance, if you're tempted by the latest sneakers, waiting a day could give you the chance to look up reviews or check if they'll go on sale soon. Practicing this can save you from a lot of regret later on.

Comparing prices online is another powerful tool in the fight against impulsive spending. Thanks to various apps and websites, it's now easier than ever to ensure you're getting the best bang for your buck. Before making any purchase, take a few minutes to search for the item across different retailers. Websites like Amazon and eBay, or price comparison tools like Honey and PriceGrabber, can show you a range of prices from different sellers.

For example, if you're eyeing a new phone, plug in its model number on multiple websites to see where it's being sold cheapest. Retailers often have varying discounts and promotions, so a little bit of homework can lead to significant savings. Plus, if you're committed to finding the best deal, it can serve as a deterrent to spur-of-the-moment buys. When you know you're getting the most value for your money, you're more likely to make thoughtful, deliberate choices.

Understanding sales tactics can also play a big role in curbing impulsive spending. Advertisers are very clever at making us feel like we need their products right now. Ever noticed those flashy "limited-time offer" banners or "only 3 left in stock" warnings? They're designed to create a sense of urgency, pushing you towards making quick decisions without adequate reflection. Being aware of these tactics helps you resist the pressure they create.

For instance, a common trick is the "buy one, get one free" promotion. While it might seem like a great deal, ask yourself if you really need two of the same item. Another example is the end-cap displays in stores, which often feature high-margin products that the retailer wants to move quickly. Don't fall for these traps. Focus on your personal needs, not the marketer's agenda. It's all about making informed choices that align with your financial goals, rather than being swayed by slick advertising.

One hidden culprit behind many impulse purchases is social media. Platforms like Instagram and TikTok are filled with influencers showcasing the latest must-have products, making it incredibly tempting to click "buy now." To combat this, carefully curate your social media feed. Unfollow accounts that consistently tempt you with products you don't need. You might even consider removing certain shopping apps from your phone or setting time limits for using them. This reduces the constant exposure to shopping triggers and helps you save money.

Another essential tip is to prioritize your financial goals. Envision your ideal financial future and set clear, specific targets. Instead of vaguely saying you want to save money, aim for something concrete, like saving $1,000 for a summer trip or setting aside $500 for a new laptop. Having these goals in mind can help you weigh the long-term benefits against the short-term gratification of an impulse buy. Each time you're tempted to make a purchase, ask yourself how it will impact your progress towards these goals. Will that trendy jacket bring you closer to your dream vacation? Probably not. But skipping it might mean reaching your savings target faster.

If you're someone who enjoys the tactile feeling of handing over cash, try paying with cash instead of using cards. Budget exactly how much you can spend on your purchases and withdraw that amount. Paying with cash can make the transaction feel more real, helping you avoid overspending. Research shows that people spend less when they use cash because the physical act of handing over money makes them more conscious of the cost (Bennett, 2023).

Recognizing signs of impulsive spending habits is key. Do you often find yourself hiding purchases from family or feeling guilty afterward? Are you spending beyond your means or unable to save because of high spending elsewhere? Pay attention to these signals, as they're indicators that you might need to reassess your spending habits.

Alright, so we've covered a lot in this chapter about managing your money like a pro. From knowing your income and expenses to setting realistic goals, you've got the basics down. Remember, budgeting isn't just about being frugal; it's about making sure you can enjoy life's little splurges without emptying your pockets. And hey, with all those handy apps at your fingertips, staying on top of your finances has never been easier!

Keep in mind that your financial journey doesn't stop here. Regularly reviewing and tweaking your budget is key to staying flexible and prepared for whatever life throws at you. It's all about finding that balance between saving for those big dreams and still having fun along the way. So go ahead, set those goals, use those tools, and make your money work for you. You've got this!

CHAPTER 8

TIME MANAGEMENT AND PRODUCTIVITY

Time Management and Productivity

Feel like you're constantly racing against the clock? Managing your time and boosting productivity doesn't have to feel like juggling flaming torches while riding a unicycle! This chapter has got you covered with super practical strategies to help you balance schoolwork, hang out with friends, and even squeeze in some downtime with your favorite book or TV show. Life can get pretty hectic when you're trying to juggle academics, social activities, and personal time. But with the right tools, you'll become a time management ninja in no time!

In this chapter, we're going to dive into techniques that make managing your time as easy (and fun) as possible. You'll learn how to set goals that aren't just dreams scribbled in your notebook but actual plans you can follow and achieve. We'll cover how to create schedules that fit your lifestyle without making you feel like you're living by a military clock. And of course, we'll tackle the beast known as procrastination, helping you conquer it once and for all. By the end, you'll not only know how to get more done but also how to enjoy your free time guilt-free. So, grab a snack, get comfy, and let's get started on turning you into a productivity master!

Setting SMART Goals

Let's dive straight into understanding how to create specific, measurable, achievable, relevant, and time-bound (SMART) goals. These types of goals are designed to set a clear direction for your activities and priorities, making it easier to balance academic, personal, and social commitments.

Understanding SMART Criteria

The SMART criteria make goal-setting straightforward and effective. Here's what each component stands for:

- **Specific**: A specific goal clearly defines what you want to achieve. It answers questions like who, what, where, when, and why. For instance, instead of saying "I want to do well in school," a specific goal would be "I want to improve my math grade from a C to a B by the end of the semester."

- **Measurable**: This means that you can track your progress. Measurable goals often include numbers or other quantifiable elements. For example, "I will read 30 pages of my history textbook every day" is measurable.

- **Achievable**: Your goal should be realistic and attainable. It's important to set a goal that challenges you but is still within reach. For instance, aiming to increase your math grade by one letter might be more achievable than trying to go from an F to an A+ in a short period.

- **Relevant**: The goal should matter to you and align with other plans you have. If your main focus this year is improving your grades, then a goal like "I will complete all my homework assignments on time" is relevant.

- **Time-bound**: Every goal needs a deadline. Having a timeframe creates urgency and prompts action. An example could be: "I will improve my math grade from a C to a B by the end of the semester," giving you a clear endpoint.

Examples of SMART Goals

To make things clearer, let's look at some relatable examples of SMART goals from teen life:

1. Learning a New Skill
- **Specific**: I want to learn how to play the guitar.
- **Measurable**: I will practice for 30 minutes every day.
- **Achievable**: I already have a guitar and access to online tutorials.
- **Relevant**: Learning the guitar is something I've always wanted to do, and it can help me relax after school.
- **Time-bound**: I will be able to play four songs proficiently within three months.

2. Improving Grades
- **Specific**: I want to improve my science grade.
- **Measurable**: I will aim for at least an 80% on all quizzes and tests.
- **Achievable**: I'm committed to spending an extra hour studying science twice a week.
- **Relevant**: Better grades in science will help me qualify for the advanced class next year.
- **Time-bound**: I will reach my goal by the end of the current semester.

3. Fitness Goal
- **Specific**: I want to run a 5K race.
- **Measurable**: I will train by running three times a week, increasing my distance by half a kilometer every two weeks.
- **Achievable**: I have running shoes, and there's a park nearby where I can train.
- **Relevant**: Running keeps me healthy and helps me manage stress.
- **Time-bound**: I will be ready for the 5K race taking place in four months.

Creating Personal SMART Goals

Now that you understand the basics, let's guide you through crafting your own SMART goals. Start by identifying something you genuinely want to accomplish. Here's a step-by-step guideline:

1. **Identify the Goal**: Think about what you want to achieve. Be as specific as possible.

2. **Make it Measurable**: Determine how you can track progress. What metrics will indicate success?

3. **Evaluate Achievability**: Is this goal realistic given your current resources and constraints? Adjust if necessary.

4. **Ensure Relevance**: Ask yourself whether this goal aligns with your long-term objectives or values.

5. **Set a Deadline**: Choose a clear timeframe to keep you focused and motivated.

For example, let's say you want to improve your overall physical fitness. Here's how you can frame it using the SMART criteria:

- **Specific**: I want to increase my stamina and strength.

- **Measurable**: I will measure my progress by noting down how long I can run without stopping and how many push-ups I can do in one go.

- **Achievable**: I'll start by running three times a week and add strength training exercises once a week.

- **Relevant**: Physical fitness is important to me because it boosts my energy levels and overall well-being.

- **Time-bound**: I will increase my stamina to run 5 kilometers continuously and double my push-up count within three months.

Reviewing and Adjusting Goals

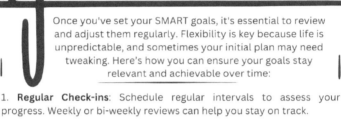

Once you've set your SMART goals, it's essential to review and adjust them regularly. Flexibility is key because life is unpredictable, and sometimes your initial plan may need tweaking. Here's how you can ensure your goals stay relevant and achievable over time:

1. **Regular Check-ins**: Schedule regular intervals to assess your progress. Weekly or bi-weekly reviews can help you stay on track.

2. **Be Honest**: If you're not making the desired progress, don't hesitate to adjust your goals. Maybe you need more time, or perhaps the goal was too ambitious.

3. **Celebrate Milestones**: Recognizing small victories along the way keeps you motivated. If you hit a milestone, give yourself a reward.

4. **Learn from Setbacks**: Instead of getting discouraged by setbacks, use them as learning opportunities. What went wrong? How can you prevent it from happening again?

Let's say you aimed to improve your grades by the end of the semester, but halfway through, you notice you're not hitting your targets. Ask yourself why. Perhaps you underestimated the amount of study time needed, or maybe unexpected events disrupted your schedule. Adjust by setting smaller, more immediate goals, like improving your quiz scores before tackling major exams.

Creating and Following a Daily Schedule

Establishing a daily routine is like building a solid foundation for your productivity house. Imagine trying to balance all those academic tasks, personal hobbies, and social activities without a plan. It would be total chaos! So, let's talk about why scheduling is super important for keeping your life on track.

First off, daily scheduling is essential because it helps you figure out what needs to get done and when. Think of it as a map guiding you through your day. When you know exactly what you're supposed to do at each hour, it's much easier to stay focused and avoid distractions. Plus, seeing everything laid out in front of you can make even the busiest day feel manageable. It's like having a cheat sheet for life!

So, now that we know why scheduling is crucial, let's dive into the tools you can use to get started. There are tons of options—some old-school, some high-tech. If you love the feel of pen and paper, a good old planner or a bullet journal might be your go-to. You'd be amazed how satisfying it is to physically check things off your list. On the other hand, if you're glued to your phone (and let's be real, who isn't?), there are plenty of apps designed to keep you organized. Apps like Google Calendar or Todoist can send you reminders and help you carve out chunks of time for different tasks. Whether you prefer scribbles in a notebook or tapping on a screen, there's definitely something that will work for you.

Alright, so you've got your tools. Now, how do you actually create an effective schedule? Buckle up, because we're going to break it down step-by-step.

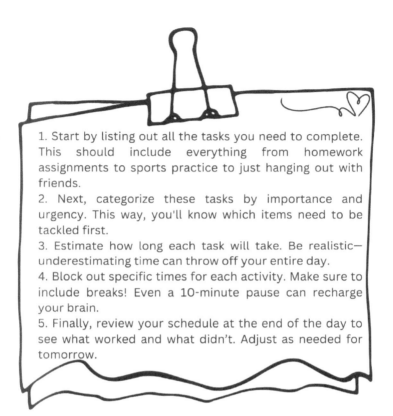

1. Start by listing out all the tasks you need to complete. This should include everything from homework assignments to sports practice to just hanging out with friends.
2. Next, categorize these tasks by importance and urgency. This way, you'll know which items need to be tackled first.
3. Estimate how long each task will take. Be realistic—underestimating time can throw off your entire day.
4. Block out specific times for each activity. Make sure to include breaks! Even a 10-minute pause can recharge your brain.
5. Finally, review your schedule at the end of the day to see what worked and what didn't. Adjust as needed for tomorrow.

Creating a schedule is one thing, but sticking to it is a whole other ball game. We've all been there: the day starts great, and then a YouTube rabbit hole eats up your study time. So, how do you make sure you stick to your schedule?

One trick is to set reminders on your phone or watch. Gentle nudges throughout the day can keep you on track. Another strategy is to break your tasks into smaller, more manageable chunks. Instead of studying for two hours straight, try 25 minutes of focused work followed by a five-minute break—a method known as the Pomodoro Technique. It makes tasks seem less daunting and keeps your brain fresh.

Accountability partners can also be incredibly helpful. Find a friend who's also trying to manage their time better and check in with each other. Knowing someone else is counting on you can be a powerful motivator. And remember, it's okay to reward yourself! Finished all your tasks for the day? Treat yourself to an episode of your favorite show or a yummy snack.

Another key point is flexibility. Life happens, and sometimes things don't go according to plan. Maybe you have an unexpected assignment or your best friend really needs to talk. That's fine! Just go back to your schedule and adjust. Being flexible doesn't mean slacking off—it means being adaptable and resilient.

Techniques to Beat Procrastination

Understanding Procrastination

Okay, let's start with understanding what's up with procrastination. It's like when you know you should be doing your homework but suddenly find yourself deep-diving into cute cat videos or scrolling through memes for hours. Makes no sense, right? Well, procrastination often happens because we're afraid of failing, not knowing where to start, or simply feeling overwhelmed.

Envision this scenario: You have a big essay due in a week. The deadline seems so far away that you push it out of your mind and do other stuff instead. As the deadline gets closer, your anxiety kicks in, making you cram all the work into one night. Stress levels shoot up, and the quality of your work takes a hit. This cycle leads to regret and promises to do better next time—but without a game plan, you're back to cat videos the next time around.

Effective Techniques to Combat Procrastination

Now, let's tackle how to kick procrastination to the curb. First up, time management techniques like the Eisenhower Box can help you prioritize tasks by sorting them into four categories: urgent and important, important but not urgent, urgent but not important, and neither urgent nor important. This way, you can focus on what truly matters. Create a daily routine that factors in these priorities, and before you know it, you'll be checking off items like a pro. Another cool trick is the 2-minute rule. If something takes less than two minutes—whether it's washing a dish or replying to an email—do it immediately. Feels good knocking those small tasks out quickly!

Also, breaking down complex assignments into smaller steps can make them feel way more manageable. Instead of thinking about writing a 2,000-word essay, start with a 100-word introduction first. Baby steps! Speaking of which, setting tiny, achievable goals and celebrating when you reach them can seriously boost your motivation. Maybe treat yourself to some chocolate or an extra ten minutes on Instagram—whatever floats your boat.

Creating Accountability

Accountability is your new best friend in fighting procrastination. When you know someone's got their eye on your progress, you're less likely to slack off. Start by clearly defining your goals and sharing them with someone you trust. This person could be a friend, family member, or even a study buddy. They'll help keep you on track and give you the nudge you need when you're veering off course.

You might even consider using apps designed for accountability partners. These tools can remind you of deadlines and let others see your progress. Plus, they can send encouraging messages to keep you motivated. But hey, remember to also hold yourself accountable. Track your progress with a journal or an app. Reflect on what worked and what didn't, making adjustments as needed.

Mindfulness and Focus Techniques

For our final magic trick, let's chat about mindfulness. Believe it or not, mindfulness practices like meditation can make a huge difference in enhancing focus and crushing procrastination. Mindful breathing exercises can help calm your brain, reducing stress and making it easier to concentrate.

Another awesome technique is focusing on one thing at a time. Seriously, multitasking is overrated. It splits your attention and makes it harder to complete tasks efficiently. Next time you're studying, avoid the temptation to check your phone or browse social media. Instead, dedicate specific times for breaks and stick to them.

There's also something to be said about creating the right environment. A clutter-free space can do wonders for your focus. Add a bit of nature with a small plant or some calming music to really set the mood. For further concentration, noise-cancelling headphones can block out distractions, putting you in the zone.

Balancing Schoolwork with Social Activities

Balancing schoolwork with social life might sound like trying to walk a tightrope while juggling flaming torches, but it's not just possible—it's necessary. Picture this: you've got a huge algebra test coming up, and your best friend is begging you to go to her birthday party. How do you decide what to prioritize? The key is balance. Striking a healthy balance between academic responsibilities and social lives ensures that you can thrive both personally and academically.

Importance of Balance

Let's start with why balancing schoolwork with your social life is crucial. Imagine if you only focused on academics. Sure, you might ace all your tests and assignments, but what's the point if you're constantly stressed out and never see your friends? On the other hand, if you're partying all the time and neglecting your schoolwork, you'll quickly find yourself falling behind, leading to stress and anxiety.

Maintaining balance helps keep you happy and healthy. You'll find that when you're not overburdened with homework, you're more refreshed and motivated. And when you're not overly consumed by social activities, you're better able to focus on important tasks. This balanced approach ultimately leads to better mental health, improved academic performance, and more fulfilling social interactions.

Strategies for Balance

Now, onto the practical part: how do you actually achieve this balance? Here are some tried-and-true strategies:

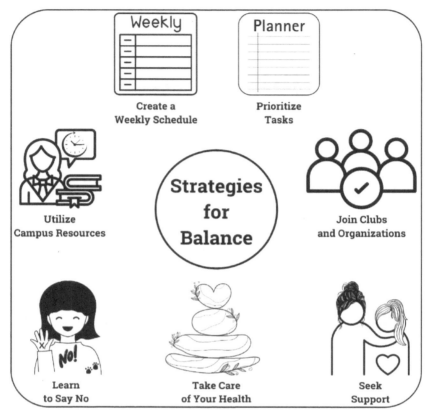

Create a Weekly Schedule: Plan your week in advance, allocating specific times for classes, study sessions, and social activities. For instance, pencil in study time right after school when your brain is still in learning mode, and save your evenings for hanging out with friends or family.

Prioritize Tasks: Identify your most critical academic tasks and tackle them first. Warren, a student from William Peace University, suggests using a planner to keep track of assignments, exams, and social events. According to her, it's about "time management and prioritizing tasks" (<i>How to Balance Academics and Social Life in

College: Tips from a William Peace University Student | William Peace University</i>, 2023). Once you've completed your schoolwork, you can enjoy your social life without that nagging feeling of unfinished tasks.

Utilize Campus Resources: Take advantage of resources like academic advisors and student organizations. These resources help you stay organized and connect you with people who share similar interests. Warren credits her success to WPU's Office of Academic and Career Advising, which helped her manage her time effectively.

Join Clubs and Organizations: Being part of after-school clubs not only helps you make friends but also gives you scheduled social activities that don't interfere with your academic commitments. Plus, many clubs offer opportunities to develop leadership skills, which look great on college applications.

Learn to Say No: While it's tempting to say yes to every social invitation, sometimes you need to prioritize your health and academics. Politely decline social events when you have pressing assignments or tests. This doesn't mean becoming a hermit; it means choosing wisely.

Take Care of Your Health: A balanced diet, regular exercise, and sufficient sleep are crucial. It's hard to balance anything if you're tired and run down. Make sure to include downtime in your schedule for self-care. Using breaks wisely to relax and recharge can make a significant difference.

Seek Support: Don't hesitate to reach out to teachers, counselors, or advisors if you're struggling to maintain balance. They can offer valuable advice and support to help you get back on track.

Effective Communication

Another essential aspect of balancing schoolwork and social life is effective communication. Openly discussing your time commitments with friends, family, and even teachers can help you manage expectations and avoid misunderstandings.

Communicate with Friends and Family: Letting your friends know you have to study for an upcoming test can prevent hurt feelings if you have to decline an invitation. Similarly, talking with your family about your schedule can ensure they understand when you need quiet time to focus.

Engage with Teachers: Don't be afraid to communicate with your teachers if you're overwhelmed. They may offer extensions, extra help, or alternative assignments to help you manage your workload better. Open dialogue fosters a supportive environment where you feel comfortable seeking assistance.

Recognizing Signs of Imbalance

Even with the best intentions and plans, life can throw curveballs that disrupt your balance. Recognizing the signs of imbalance can help you take corrective action before things spiral out of control.

Signs of Academic Imbalance: If you find yourself consistently pulling all-nighters, missing deadlines, or feeling overwhelmed by schoolwork, it's a sign that you need to re-evaluate your balance. Maybe you've taken on too much or need to improve your time management skills.

Signs of Social Imbalance: On the flip side, if you notice that you're isolated, haven't hung out with friends in weeks, or are feeling lonely and disconnected, it's time to re-prioritize your social life. Social interactions are crucial for mental well-being, so make an effort to schedule some fun activities.

Physical Symptoms: Often, your body will tell you when something's off. Constant fatigue, frequent headaches, or general malaise could indicate stress from poor balance. Pay attention to these signals and adjust accordingly.

Adjusting Focus

When you recognize signs of imbalance, it's essential to adjust your focus. This could mean tweaking your schedule, making more time for self-care, or seeking help.

Reevaluate Your Priorities: Sometimes, you need to step back and reassess what's truly important. Are there extracurricular activities you can cut back on? Do you need to ask for help with a challenging subject?

Flexibility is Key: Understand that perfection isn't the goal—balance is. Be flexible and willing to change your plans as needed. Unexpected things happen, and being adaptable ensures you stay balanced even when things don't go as planned.

Balancing your academic life, personal hobbies, and social activities can feel like trying to juggle flaming torches while riding a unicycle. But, with the techniques we've explored, such as setting SMART goals and creating an effective daily schedule, you can conquer the chaos. Remember, specificity in your goals will keep you focused, and measurable milestones will give you that extra boost of motivation. Flexibility is crucial—life has its way of throwing curveballs, but adjusting your plans doesn't mean you're failing; it means you're learning to adapt like a pro.

Taking charge of procrastination by breaking tasks into smaller, manageable steps can turn those big scary projects into bite-sized victories. And let's not forget about striking the perfect balance between schoolwork and hanging out with friends. A well-rounded schedule that includes time for both study and fun keeps you happy, healthy, and ready to tackle any challenge thrown your way. So go ahead, craft those SMART goals, rock that daily schedule, and show procrastination who's in charge.

you've GOT THIS

CHAPTER 9

MENTAL HEALTH AND WELLBEING

Mental Health and Wellbeing

Have you ever felt like keeping your mental health in check is as tricky as walking a tightrope? It's all about skill, balance, and a whole lot of practice! In this chapter, we're diving deep into the world of stress and anxiety—those unwelcome guests that seem to pop up right when you're trying to relax. But don't worry; recognizing their sneaky signs is half the battle. Do you sometimes get a headache after a tough day at school? That's your body's way of saying it's time to hit pause, slow down, and give yourself some well-deserved self-care.

Once you've got a handle on spotting these not-so-subtle signals from your body, we'll move onto decoding your emotions. Spoiler alert: it's totally normal to feel irritable or sad sometimes—you're not turning into a drama queen! Understanding these emotional cues can be a game-changer. It's like getting a cheat code for managing pre-exam jitters or handling drama with friends. We're also throwing in a mix of practical strategies to help you build a rock-solid coping toolkit. From problem-solving techniques to the soothing art of journaling, we've got your back. And hey, if things ever get too overwhelming, knowing when to chat with a professional can make all the difference. Get ready to tackle stress head-on and reclaim your calm, one deep breath at a time!

Recognizing Signs of Stress and Anxiety

Understanding stress and anxiety is crucial, especially for teenage girls who are facing an array of life pressures. Recognizing your own signs of stress is the first step in managing it effectively. Let's dive into how you can identify these signs and what they might mean for you.

Your body often gives you clear signals when you're stressed. Have you ever noticed a headache creeping in after a tough day at school or felt utterly exhausted without doing much? These are common physical symptoms of stress. Your body reacts to mental strain just like it does to physical exertion. Headaches, fatigue, and even stomachaches are your body's way of telling you that it's time to slow down and take care of yourself. Keeping an eye on these symptoms helps you become more attuned to your body's needs. When you notice these signs, it's a good cue to engage in some self-care activities, whether that's taking a break, going for a walk, or just lounging with a good book.

Now, let's talk feelings. Emotions can be tricky and sometimes we don't even realize we're stressed until someone points it out. Irritability, feeling sad for no apparent reason, or becoming easily overwhelmed are emotional indicators of stress. It's completely normal to have these feelings, especially during stressful times. By acknowledging them, you are not just validating your emotions but also taking a big step towards constructive self-awareness. Think about it – if you know that you're likely to get irritable before exams, you can plan ahead to manage those feelings better. Maybe practice some relaxation techniques or ensure you get enough rest beforehand. Being aware of your emotional responses allows you to tackle them head-on, making it easier to maintain balance.

Behavioral changes often tell us what our thoughts and emotions might not. Have you found yourself sleeping less, waking up in the middle of the night, or wanting to sleep all the time? Or maybe you've noticed that you're withdrawing from friends and family? Changes in sleeping patterns and social interactions are significant behavioral indicators of stress. If you're staying up late scrolling through your phone or avoiding social gatherings, it might be time to reflect on what's causing that behavior. Sometimes talking about what's stressing you out with someone you trust can make a world of difference. It opens up space for proactive discussions about mental health and encourages a supportive environment where you don't have to deal with things alone.

One fantastic tool for managing stress and identifying its triggers is journaling. Writing down your thoughts and feelings helps you track patterns and see what exactly is stressing you out. Not only does it serve as a form of self-reflection, but it also provides a safe place to express yourself without fear of judgment. You can jot down how you feel each day, note any physical symptoms, and reflect on your emotional state. Over time, you might start seeing connections between certain events or behaviors and your stress levels. This awareness empowers you to take actionable steps towards better mental health. For instance, if you notice a spike in stress every time you have a math test, you could try studying in smaller, more manageable chunks instead of cramming the night before. Guidelines for effective journaling include setting aside a specific time each day for writing, being honest with your entries, and not worrying about grammar or spelling – this is your personal space.

Another essential point is recognizing that everyone experiences stress differently. What might be a minor inconvenience for one person could be a major stressor for another. Understanding your unique reactions to stress means you can develop personalized coping strategies that work best for you. This individuality extends to solutions as well. Some people find solace in physical activities like running or dancing, while others might prefer quieter activities like reading or crafting. The key is to experiment and find out what reduces your stress most effectively.

Creating a balanced lifestyle also plays a significant role in managing stress. Regular physical activity, a healthy diet, sufficient sleep, and positive social interactions are fundamental components. Eating right fuels your body, making it better equipped to handle stress (Cleveland Clinic, 2024). Engaging in regular physical activity releases endorphins, which naturally combat stress. Ensuring you get enough sleep helps regulate your mood and keeps you energized throughout the day (Mayo Clinic, 2023).

Sometimes, despite all efforts, stress can feel overwhelming. It's crucial to recognize when it's time to seek professional help. If you find that your stress is affecting your physical health, causing persistent emotional distress, or leading you to unhealthy coping mechanisms like substance use, speaking to a healthcare provider is vital. They can guide you through various stress management techniques, offer counseling, or provide other forms of support tailored to your needs (Cleveland Clinic, 2024).

Simple Self-Care Practices

Maintaining our mental health is a bit like taking care of a plant – it needs regular watering, sunlight, and sometimes a little talking-to. As teenage girls navigating through school, friendships, social media, and family expectations, it's essential to have some easy self-care routines in your toolkit to keep that mental flora thriving. Let's dive into a few practical tips and tricks to help you stay balanced, calm, and ready to face whatever comes your way!

Physical Activity: Get Moving!

When life feels overwhelming, one of the best things you can do is get moving. Physical activity isn't just about staying fit; it has tons of benefits for your mood and overall mental health. Playing sports, going for a run, dancing around your room, or even just walking your dog can make a massive difference. When you're active, your body releases endorphins, often called the "feel-good hormones," which work magic by reducing stress and making you feel happier. So, even if you're not a sports enthusiast, try to find an activity that makes you excited to move.

Here's a guideline to help you get started:

1. **Find Your Fun:** Choose an activity you genuinely enjoy. It could be anything from skateboarding to Zumba.

2. **Set Small Goals:** Start with manageable goals like 10 minutes of activity each day, and gradually increase as you get more comfortable.

3. **Make It Social:** Invite friends to join you. Sharing the experience can motivate you and add an element of fun.

Mindfulness and Meditation: Find Your Zen

Sometimes, our minds are like monkeys bouncing from one tree to another, never settling down. Mindfulness practices and meditation can help quiet that mental chatter and bring a sense of calm and focus. Whether it's breathing exercises, guided meditations via apps, or simply taking a moment to really pay attention to the here and now, these techniques can do wonders for your mental well-being.

To start your mindfulness journey, consider this guideline:

1. **Breathe Deeply:** Begin with simple breathing exercises. Try inhaling for four counts, holding for four, and exhaling for four. Repeat a few times.

2. **Use Technology:** There are awesome apps like Headspace and Calm that offer guided meditations tailored specially for teens.

3. **Create a Routine:** Dedicate a few minutes each morning or evening to mindfulness exercises. Consistency is key!

Creative Outlets: Express Yourself

There's something incredibly therapeutic about letting your creative juices flow. Whether it's drawing, painting, writing stories, or playing an instrument, creative activities provide an outlet for expressing emotions that might be hard to put into words. They help manage stress, process feelings, and can even lead to surprising personal insights.

Follow these steps to nurture your creativity:

1. **Explore Different Mediums:** Don't stick to just one form of creativity—experiment with different activities until you find what clicks.

2. **Keep a Journal:** Write down your thoughts, doodle, or sketch. This can be a private space where you express whatever's on your mind without any judgment.

3. **Dedicate Time:** Set aside regular time for your chosen creative activity, making it an integral part of your routine.

Setting Boundaries: Me Time Matters

 Teenage years are full of demands from school, family, and friends, and it's crucial to know when to say no. Setting boundaries isn't about being selfish; it's about taking care of yourself so you can be at your best. Having 'me time' helps reduce feelings of overwhelm and promotes self-respect.

Here are some guidelines to help you set healthy boundaries:

1. **Identify Your Limits:** Be honest with yourself about what you can handle. It's okay to step back if you're feeling stretched too thin.

2. **Communicate Clearly:** Let people know when you need time for yourself. It's perfectly fine to say, "I need a break" or "I can't help with that right now."

3. **Stick to Your Plan:** Once you've set boundaries, respect them. Make sure your 'me time' is non-negotiable and protected from intrusions.

Building Coping Mechanisms and Resilience

Developing coping strategies to handle challenges and build emotional strength is crucial for maintaining mental health and overall well-being. Let's dive into a few practical ways you can tackle life's ups and downs while growing stronger emotionally.

First, let's talk about problem-solving skills. Imagine you've got a big math test coming up, and you're feeling all the stress vibes. Instead of letting the anxiety take over, break the problem down into smaller steps. You could start by reviewing what you already know, making a study plan, and maybe even asking for help from a teacher or friend. This way, instead of panicking, you're actively working towards a solution. Problem-solving isn't just for schoolwork; it's a life skill that helps turn challenges into opportunities for growth. When you approach issues with a mindset geared towards finding solutions, you build resilience and boost your confidence in seeking support when needed (Gloria & Steinhardt, 2016).

Next, let's explore healthy grieving practices. Life's tougher moments often involve dealing with loss, whether it's the passing of a loved one, a friendship ending, or missing out on something important to you. Grieving is a natural response to such losses, and it's essential to allow yourself to feel those emotions. It's okay to be sad, angry, or confused. Acknowledge these feelings rather than bottling them up. Talking to someone you trust—like a family member, friend, or counselor—can also help. They can offer support and remind you that it's normal to grieve. Over time, expressing your feelings helps you heal, making it easier to move forward.

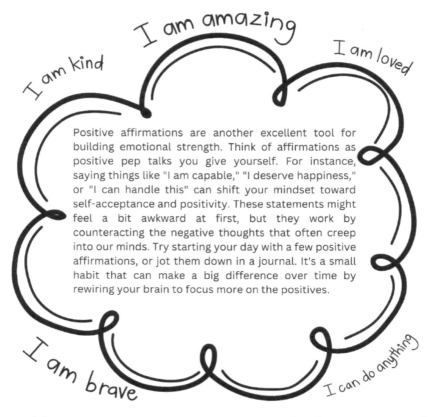

I am kind
I am amazing
I am loved
I am brave
I can do anything

Positive affirmations are another excellent tool for building emotional strength. Think of affirmations as positive pep talks you give yourself. For instance, saying things like "I am capable," "I deserve happiness," or "I can handle this" can shift your mindset toward self-acceptance and positivity. These statements might feel a bit awkward at first, but they work by counteracting the negative thoughts that often creep into our minds. Try starting your day with a few positive affirmations, or jot them down in a journal. It's a small habit that can make a big difference over time by rewiring your brain to focus more on the positives.

Maintaining strong support systems is also key to emotional well-being. Friends and family play a vital role here. Imagine having a bad day at school—maybe you bombed a test or had an argument with a friend. Instead of isolating yourself, try reaching out to someone in your support circle. Their encouragement and understanding can lighten your emotional load. Whether you meet up for a chat, call, or text, connecting with others helps validate your feelings and reminds you that you're not alone. Building these connections requires effort, like scheduling regular hangouts or simply checking in with each other, but the benefits are immense. As psychologist Barbara L. Fredrickson points out, social interactions not only alleviate feelings of isolation but also improve mood and provide emotional safety (Fredrickson, 2009).

So, how do we put these coping strategies into action? Here are some guidelines:

Problem-Solving Skills

1. **Break It Down:** When faced with a problem, deconstruct it into smaller, manageable tasks.

2. **Seek Support:** Don't hesitate to ask for help from friends, teachers, or mentors.

3. **Stay Organized:** Use planners or apps to keep track of your progress and deadlines.

4. **Reflect:** After solving a problem, take a moment to reflect on what you learned and how you handled it.

Healthy Grieving Practices

1. **Acknowledge Emotions:** Allow yourself to feel and express your emotions freely.

2. **Share with Others:** Talk about your feelings with trusted individuals.

3. **Engage in Healing Activities:** Activities like journaling, painting, or spending time in nature can be therapeutic.

4. **Seek Professional Help:** If grief becomes overwhelming, consider speaking to a counselor or therapist (Wilson, 2023).

Positive Affirmations

1. **Daily Practice:** Start your day with positive statements about yourself.

2. **Use Visual Cues:** Place sticky notes with affirmations around your room or on your mirror.

3. **Incorporate into Routine:** Integrate affirmations into your daily activities, like brushing your teeth or before bedtime.

Support Systems

1. **Build Relationships:** Make time to nurture friendships and family connections.

2. **Communicate:** Have open and honest conversations about your feelings.

3. **Participate in Social Activities:** Join clubs, groups, or activities that interest you and where you can meet supportive people.

Putting these strategies into practice doesn't have to be overwhelming. Start by choosing one area to focus on, such as using positive affirmations or improving your problem-solving skills. As you become more comfortable, you'll find that these habits blend seamlessly into your life, helping you navigate challenges with greater ease and building a stronger emotional foundation.

Seeking Professional Help When Needed

When stress and anxiety start to feel overwhelming, it's crucial not to be afraid of seeking professional help. One important step in maintaining mental health is understanding therapy and its role. Therapy isn't about lying on a couch and spilling your secrets while someone takes notes silently. It's a collaborative process that helps you work through your thoughts and emotions with a trained professional. Therapy can provide valuable tools to manage symptoms, learn coping mechanisms, and foster personal growth.

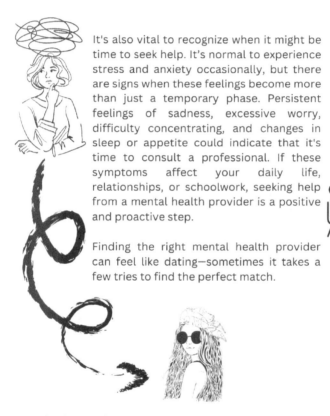

It's also vital to recognize when it might be time to seek help. It's normal to experience stress and anxiety occasionally, but there are signs when these feelings become more than just a temporary phase. Persistent feelings of sadness, excessive worry, difficulty concentrating, and changes in sleep or appetite could indicate that it's time to consult a professional. If these symptoms affect your daily life, relationships, or schoolwork, seeking help from a mental health provider is a positive and proactive step.

Finding the right mental health provider can feel like dating—sometimes it takes a few tries to find the perfect match.

But don't get discouraged! Here are some practical tips to make the search easier:

1. **Research and Referrals**: Start by asking your primary care doctor for recommendations. Friends, family members, or

even school counselors might also have suggestions. You can also look up reviews online; many therapists have profiles detailing their specializations and approaches.

2. **Credentials and Specialties**: Ensure that the therapist holds the proper credentials, such as being licensed in your state. Additionally, consider what issues you need help with—whether it's anxiety, depression, trauma, etc.—and find someone who specializes in that area.

3. **Comfort and Compatibility**: Cultural background and personal preferences matter. For instance, if you feel more comfortable talking to someone who understands your cultural background, look for therapists with similar cultural experiences or language proficiencies.

4. **Trial Sessions**: Don't be afraid to book initial consultations with a few different therapists. Most therapists understand the importance of finding the right fit and won't be offended if you decide to go with someone else after a first meeting.

Support groups are another excellent resource for those struggling with stress and anxiety. They bring together people who are facing similar challenges, providing a sense of community and mutual support. Participating in a support group can help you feel less isolated and judged. It's comforting to know you're not alone and others truly understand what you're going through.

Support groups come in various formats, including face-to-face meetings, teleconferences, or online communities. Each format has its benefits, allowing you to choose what works best for your schedule and comfort level. Some are led by laypersons—people who have shared similar experiences—while others are facilitated by professionals such as nurses or psychologists.

The benefits of joining a support group can be substantial. Firstly, you'll often feel an immediate reduction in loneliness, knowing that others share your struggles. Secondly, discussing your feelings openly in a safe environment can significantly reduce distress, depression, anxiety, or fatigue. Thirdly, you'll pick up new coping strategies and skills from others who have been where you are now.

Support groups can also function as a bridge between medical treatment and emotional support. Sometimes, the relationship with your doctor or therapist might not fully meet your emotional needs. A support group fills that gap by offering a platform to share personal experiences, coping strategies, and firsthand information about treatments and challenges.

Additionally, participating in a support group keeps you motivated to manage chronic conditions or stick to treatment plans. Members often share encouragement and practical advice that help in overcoming obstacles and staying on track. Whether it's learning how to handle a particularly tough day or celebrating small victories, a support group can boost your resilience and confidence.

In this chapter, we dived into all sorts of ways to keep stress and anxiety from taking over your life. We started with recognizing the signs – those headaches, that random sadness, or just feeling super irritable for no reason. Then, we talked about how your behavior can change when you're stressed, like sleeping too much or not enough, and pulling back from friends. Knowing these signs means you can start taking care of yourself right away with some solid self-care strategies.

We also covered how keeping a journal can help you track what's stressing you out and develop personalized coping tricks. Remember, everyone deals with stress differently, so finding what works best for you is key. Whether it's physical activity, mindfulness exercises, creative outlets, or setting firm boundaries, there's no one-size-fits-all solution. But with a balanced lifestyle and being mindful of when to seek professional help if things get really tough, you'll be better equipped to handle whatever comes your way. Keep experimenting until you find your groove!

CHAPTER 10

SOCIAL SKILLS AND COMMUNICATION

Social Skills and Communication

Does navigating social interactions sometimes feel as tricky as solving a Rubik's Cube in the dark? Don't worry, this chapter is here to guide you through the colorful maze of human communication without feeling overwhelmed. We'll break down what makes conversations truly effective and show you how to become the friend everyone trusts and turns to. Consider it your chance to level up your conversational game—learning not just to talk, but to connect on a deeper, more meaningful level.

So, what's in store for you? First, we'll explore the fine art of active listening – trust me, it's more than just nodding your head seriously while secretly planning your weekend. We'll share simple yet powerful techniques to make sure you're genuinely engaged in conversations. You'll also learn practical ways to express yourself clearly and confidently, even if public speaking currently ranks right up there with encountering a spider the size of a dinner plate. We'll discuss how to turn peer pressure into something positive, and tackle conflicts like a pro. By the end of this chapter, you'll be equipped with the tools to build stronger relationships and boost your confidence, one conversation at a time. Ready to get started? Let's jump in!

Active Listening Techniques

Imagine you're at a party with your friends, and someone is telling a story. You might be tempted to check your phone, drift into your own thoughts, or even interrupt with your own tale. But, if you really want to build strong relationships and be seen as a great friend, it's all about active listening.

 Active listening involves fully concentrating, understanding, responding, and remembering what is being said. It's not just about hearing words; it's about being genuinely engaged and present in the conversation. Think of it like this: instead of waiting for your turn to speak, you're diving into what the other person is saying with full attention. This can make them feel valued and understood which strengthens your bond.

One of the easiest ways to practice active listening is through techniques like nodding, summarizing, and asking questions. These may sound simple, but they work wonders. When your friend tells you something, nod to show you're following along. When they're done talking, you might summarize what they said by saying something like, "So, what you're saying is..." This shows you've paid attention and helps clear up any misunderstandings. Asking questions like, "How did that make you feel?" or "What happened next?" keeps the conversation going and shows you're interested.

However, let's face it – our world is jam-packed with distractions. Phone notifications, background noises, or even preconceived notions about what someone is going to say can seriously get in the way. Imagine trying to listen to your friend's story while getting constant text messages. Impossible, right? Turning off notifications during conversations can help you stay focused. Also, try to set aside any judgments or assumptions about what the other person is saying. If you go into a conversation thinking you already know what they'll say, you might miss out on important details or misunderstand their feelings.

Non-verbal signals play a massive role in active listening too. Eye contact, for instance, can make a huge difference. Looking someone in the eye shows you're genuinely interested and paying attention. But remember, too much eye contact can be intense, so balance it out. Leaning slightly towards the speaker or mimicking their body language subtly can also indicate you're engaged. Just don't overdo it – you want to come across as naturally interested, not like a mime!

Now, let's talk about some hiccups you might face. Distracted listening is a biggie. It's when you're physically there but mentally elsewhere. Maybe you're stressing over homework or daydreaming about an upcoming trip. To combat this, take a deep breath and refocus on the person speaking. It helps to remind yourself why the conversation matters to you and how it benefits your friendship.

Another roadblock is preconceived notions. If you think you already know what someone will say, you might tune out or prepare your response while they're still talking. This not only disrupts the flow of conversation but can lead to misunderstandings. Instead, approach each conversation with curiosity. Even if you think you know the gist, there's always more to learn.

Building on this, one important aspect of active listening often overlooked is the power of pausing. Have you ever been in a chat where it felt like a race to get the words out? Taking a moment before responding can give you time to process what's been said and think about your reply. It shows you're considering their words carefully, which can mean a lot to the speaker.

Sometimes, despite your best efforts, the other person might seem uninterested or distracted. Here, it's essential to recognize when it's best to exit the conversation gracefully. Saying something like, "I can see you're busy right now. Let's catch up later," respects their time and prevents you from feeling ignored.

If you find listening challenging, professional help can be a game-changer. Therapists, social skills training, or self-help books on interpersonal skills can provide strategies tailored to your needs. And hey, practice makes perfect. Like learning to ride a bike, becoming good at active listening takes time and effort. Keep practicing, be patient with yourself, and soon you'll notice positive changes in your interactions.

Remember, practicing active listening doesn't just benefit you. When people see you genuinely listening, they may be inspired to do the same. Your efforts can create a ripple effect, leading to more meaningful and connected conversations all around.

Lastly, don't underestimate the value of active listening in different settings. Whether you're at school, home, or hanging out with friends, mastering this skill can enhance your relationships and boost your confidence. By continually practicing these techniques, active listening will become second nature. You'll start to ask open-ended questions and reflect what you've heard without even thinking about it.

Expressing Yourself Clearly and Confidently

Articulating your thoughts and feelings effectively is like magic; it can boost your confidence and make you feel like a communication wizard in various situations. Let's dive into some practical ways to make this happen.

First things first, keep it simple. Using plain language and structuring your thoughts logically can work wonders for clarity. Imagine you're trying to explain something to a friend. If you use complicated words or jump from one idea to another without any flow, your friend might get lost or lose interest. For instance, instead of saying, "I was experiencing an epiphany about the existential nature of our reality," you could say, "I realized something important about life." See how much easier that is to understand? Plus, it makes you sound more approachable and genuine.

Next, let's talk about practice. No, not the kind of practice where you just think about what you're going to say, but real, actual speaking practice. One cool trick is to practice in front of a mirror. Yes, it might feel a bit silly at first, but it helps! When you see yourself talking, you become aware of your body language, facial expressions, and gestures. You can adjust these to seem more confident and engaging. Similarly, recording yourself speaking can be incredibly helpful. When you play it back, pay attention to your tone, speed, and clarity. Are you mumbling? Talking too fast? Sounding robotic? These recordings will give you insights on areas to improve. And don't worry, even the best speakers started out feeling awkward!

Then, there's the big, scary monster: public speaking fear. Guess what? Most people are naturally empathetic. Your audience isn't a group of critics ready to pounce on every mistake. They're human beings who generally want to see you succeed. Knowing this can take a huge load off your shoulders. Instead of imagining everyone in the audience as harsh judges, think of them as friends who are genuinely interested in what you have to say. This shift in perspective can make speaking in front of others feel a lot less daunting.

Now, here's a game-changer: seek constructive criticism. Asking for feedback might sound intimidating, but it's one of the best ways to improve. Think of it like playing a video game—you need to know where you're going wrong to get better. Ask a trusted friend, family member, or even a mentor to listen to you speak or read something you've written. Ask them specific questions like, "Did I come across clearly?" or "Was my message easy to understand?" Reflecting on their feedback can give you new strategies and perspectives to refine your communication skills. It's like having a personalized guide to becoming a better speaker!

Okay, let's bring all these ideas together with a practical guideline that incorporates what we've talked about.

Guideline for Confident Speaking:

1 — **Simplify Your Language**: Break down complex thoughts into simple terms. Use short sentences and everyday words to make your points clear.

2 — **Logical Structure**: Organize your main points logically—start with an introduction, follow up with supporting details, and wrap up with a conclusion.

3 — **Mirror Practice**: Stand in front of a mirror and deliver your speech. Watch your facial expressions, gestures, and posture.

4 — **Record Yourself**: Use your smartphone or computer to record your speech. Listen carefully to identify issues with tone, speed, and clarity.

5 — **Audience Empathy**: Remember that your audience wants you to do well. Visualize them as supportive friends rather than critical judges.

6 — **Seek Constructive Criticism**: After practicing, ask someone you trust for feedback. Focus on specific areas for improvement.

Dealing with Peer Pressure Constructively

Recognizing that peer pressure can be both positive and negative is crucial for decision-making. We all know the typical image of peer pressure: sneaky friends trying to get you to do something you shouldn't. But guess what? Not all peer pressure is bad! Sometimes, your friends can actually push you towards healthy competition, like joining a new club or trying a new hobby. That's the positive kind of peer pressure, and it's something we should all appreciate.

But let's face it, the not-so-fun kind is when someone tries to coerce you into doing things that make you uncomfortable or that go against your values. The tricky part is recognizing which is which. Just because everyone else is diving off the cliff doesn't mean you have to—especially if you know you're scared of heights! Understanding these differences helps you make better choices, knowing when to jump in and when to just chill by the sidelines with a cold lemonade.

Having a set of personal values can act as a guide for making choices and creating refusal strategies. Think of your personal values as your internal GPS. They help you navigate through life's tricky roads. If you've got a strong sense of what's important to you—whether it's honesty, kindness, or staying true to yourself—you'll find it much easier to say "no" when someone tries to steer you off course.

For example, let's say your value is being honest. If someone asks you to copy their homework, your internal GPS will remind you that this goes against your belief. You can then say, "No, I'm not comfortable with that," and stick to your guns. Creating refusal strategies ahead of time can also save you from those awkward on-the-spot decisions.

How about practicing saying "no" with a friend? Make it fun, like a mini-drama session where you take turns convincing each other to do silly but harmless things and then practice politely refusing. This way, when real-life situations come knocking, you'll be ready!

Engaging with peers who encourage growth can help transform pressure into positive experiences. Imagine you're climbing a mountain. Wouldn't you prefer to climb with friends who cheer you on, rather than those who try to trip you up? Surround yourself with people who inspire you to be your best self. These are the friends who'll say, "Hey, wanna join me in trying out for the school play?" instead of "Let's skip class today."

Positive peer influence can motivate you to explore new interests and develop new skills. These friends respect your boundaries and celebrate your successes. When you're surrounded by uplifting people, even challenges become opportunities for growth. For instance, if your buddy has a strict study schedule, you might feel inspired to create one too. Isn't it amazing how the right crowd can turn pressure into motivation?

Sharing and reflecting on experiences with peer pressure can highlight personal patterns and values. Talking about your experiences with peer pressure can be incredibly eye-opening. Start a conversation with your friends about moments when they felt pressured and how they dealt with it. Hearing different perspectives can show you that you're not alone and that everyone faces similar challenges.

Reflecting on past experiences, either by talking or journaling, lets you identify patterns in your behavior. Do you always give in when the pressure becomes too much? Or maybe you tend to stand firm on certain values while compromising on others. By highlighting these patterns, you can work on strengthening your resolve in weak areas.

Additionally, sharing your experiences helps others learn from your mistakes or victories. It's a win-win! Reflecting can also reinforce your values. When you see how sticking to your beliefs has kept you out of trouble or brought you success, you'll feel more confident about doing it again in the future.

So, next time you're chilling with your friends, bring up the topic. Share funny stories, serious moments, and everything in between. You might just end up learning something new about yourself and your buddies.

Navigating Conflict Resolution

Alright, let's dive right in! Conflicts happen to all of us. They're a natural part of any relationship, but it's how we handle them that really matters. Recognizing that conflicts are as natural as breathing can actually help lessen the negativity you feel when they arise. Instead of thinking, "Oh no, here we go again," you can start seeing conflicts as opportunities for growth and better understanding between people.

So, how do you tackle these conflicts in a way that leaves everyone feeling respected? One great technique is using 'I' statements. This isn't about turning into a robot who starts every sentence with "I think" or "I feel," but rather shifting from accusatory language to more personal expressions. Instead of saying, "You always ignore me," try, "I feel really hurt when I don't get a response." See? It shifts the focus from blaming the other person to expressing your own feelings, which makes it easier for the other person to understand where you're coming from without getting defensive.

LIFE SKILLS PLAYBOOK FOR TEEN GIRLS

Speaking of understanding, active listening is super important during conflicts. Often, we're so focused on what we want to say next that we don't really hear what the other person is saying. Active listening means fully concentrating on the speaker, understanding their message, responding thoughtfully, and remembering what was said. This can be as simple as nodding, summarizing what you've heard, or asking questions like, "What did you mean when you said...?" These small actions show that you value the other person's perspective and are genuinely trying to understand them.

But let's be real: sometimes, despite our best efforts, emotions can run high during conflicts. This is where deep breathing exercises and taking timeouts come in handy. When you feel your frustration building up, take a few slow, deep breaths. It might sound too simple to work, but deep breathing helps reduce stress and gives you a moment to think before you react. And if deep breathing isn't cutting it, don't be afraid to call a timeout. Just make sure to communicate that you need a break and set a time to revisit the conversation later. Something like, "I need a few minutes to calm down. Can we talk about this again at 4 PM?" This not only helps you manage your emotions but also shows respect for the other person's feelings.

Now, some conflicts can get pretty heated, and there may come a point when you realize you can't resolve it on your own. That's when knowing when to seek help becomes crucial. Trusted adults, like parents, teachers, or school counselors, can offer valuable perspectives or mediate the situation effectively. In more serious cases, mediation through professional counselors or therapists could be necessary. It's important to recognize that asking for help doesn't mean you're failing; it means you're committed to resolving the conflict in the healthiest way possible.

Let's walk through an example. Imagine you and your best friend have had a massive argument over something trivial—like who gets to sit in the front seat of the car. Initially, it feels like the end of the world. But remember, conflicts are natural. Start by sharing your feelings using 'I' statements. You might say, "I felt really left out when you took the front seat." Pay attention to their side of the story by actively listening. Maybe they respond with, "I didn't realize it meant so much to you. I just wanted to sit up front because I felt nauseous in the back."

Next, try to stay calm. Take a deep breath and suggest a timeout if needed. After calming down, revisit the conflict at a designated time and see if a compromise can be reached. If things escalate or can't be settled, don't hesitate to involve a trusted adult who can help mediate the situation.

To wrap things up, it's essential to see conflicts as opportunities for growth rather than setbacks. Utilizing 'I' statements and active listening fosters mutual understanding and respect. Managing your emotions through deep breathing and timeouts keeps the conversation constructive. And knowing when to seek external help ensures that conflicts are resolved in the most effective way. Mastering these techniques will equip you to handle conflicts constructively, leading to healthier and stronger relationships.

Wow, we've covered a lot in this chapter, haven't we? From mastering the art of active listening to expressing ourselves with wizard-like clarity and dealing with peer pressure like pros, we've got it all down. Remember how we talked about making eye contact without turning into a staring contest champion? And who knew that simply nodding along could make you a better friend? Plus, handling sneaky distractions and those pesky preconceived notions is no easy feat, but hey, we've got our strategies lined up!

As we wrap things up, let's take a moment to appreciate how these skills can transform our interactions. Whether it's pausing to truly listen or finding the guts to speak confidently, these tools are like superpowers for any setting —school, home, or hanging out with pals. So go on, practice away! You might just start turning heads (and hearts) with your newfound communication mojo. Keep at it, and soon you'll be the go-to guru for navigating the tricky world of conversations and relationships.

CHAPTER 11

SAFE DIGITAL SKILLS

Safe Digital Skills

What if you could navigate the digital world like a pro, knowing your personal information is safe and your online experience is always positive? Mastering the internet isn't just about browsing or posting on social media—it's about learning key online safety tips that keep you secure. Want to know how to create hacker-proof passwords? Curious about what two-factor authentication really means? In this chapter, we'll dive into these topics in a fun and easy-to-understand way, helping you boost your online superpowers one tip at a time!

We'll start with creating strong, unique passwords to fend off hackers and protect your identity. Then, you'll get introduced to password managers – think of them as your digital BFFs. They help keep your passwords safe, so you don't have to stress about remembering them all. Plus, we'll dive into the importance of two-factor authentication, adding an extra layer of security to your accounts. Finally, we'll talk about keeping tabs on your personal information and staying alert for any suspicious activity. By the end of this chapter, you'll have all the skills you need to navigate the digital landscape safely and confidently!

Creating Strong Passwords and Protecting Your Identity

Ever thought about how to keep your online life safe? In this digital age, knowing how to protect your personal information is like having a superpower. This section is all about teaching you the tricks and tools to stay secure online.

First up, let's chat about passwords. Imagine if you used the same key for your house, car, locker, and diary. If someone got hold of that key, they'd have access to everything! The same goes for passwords. Using unique passwords for each account is the key to keeping hackers at bay. A lot of people make the mistake of using simple or common passwords – think "password123" or their pet's name. These are incredibly easy for hackers to guess. Instead, go for a mix of letters, numbers, and symbols to create a strong password. Not only does this make it harder for others to crack, but it also acts as a shield against identity theft.

Now, remembering all those complex passwords can be tricky. Enter password managers – your new BFF in the digital world. These nifty tools store and manage all your passwords securely, so you don't have to remember every single one. With a password manager, you only need to recall one master password to access all your accounts. Plus, they often come with features like generating strong passwords and alerting you if any of your passwords are weak or compromised. Some popular password managers include LastPass, Dashlane, and 1Password.

By using these, you'll not only enhance your security but also save time and effort. (The Importance of Password Managers for College Students, Faculty and Staff: 4 Essential Tips, 2024)

But wait, there's more to fortifying your online fortress. Let's talk about Two-Factor Authentication (2FA). Think of 2FA as an additional lock on your door. Even if someone figures out your password, they still need another piece of information to get in. This could be a code sent to your phone, your fingerprint, or even facial recognition. Enabling 2FA adds an extra layer of security, making it significantly tougher for hackers to access your accounts. Most online services offer this feature, and it's a good habit to enable it wherever possible. According to the Cybersecurity and Infrastructure Security Agency, users who enable MFA (Multi-Factor Authentication) are much less likely to get hacked because even if someone has your password, they won't have the second authentication factor (CISA, 2023).

One last thing – keeping tabs on your personal information. It's not enough to set up strong defenses; you also need to be proactive in monitoring any unusual activity. **Set up alerts** on your accounts so you're notified immediately if something seems off. Regularly review and update your **privacy settings** across all platforms. This helps you understand who can see your information and gives you control over what is shared publicly. Also, periodically **check your bank statements**, **credit reports**, and other sensitive information for any signs of suspicious activity. By staying vigilant and regularly reviewing your settings, you can catch potential threats early before they become bigger problems.

Managing Screen Time and Its Impact on Wellbeing

Recognizing Screen Time Limits

Let's start with the basics: recognizing screen time limits is super important, especially when digital devices are practically glued to our hands. Setting daily screen time limits isn't just about cutting back; it's about finding a sweet spot where technology supports our lives without taking over.

A good starting point? Many experts recommend no more than two hours of recreational screen time per day for teenagers.

So, how do you actually keep track? There are plenty of apps out there that can help monitor and control your screen time. Apps like "Screen Time" for iOS or "Digital Wellbeing" for Android give you a detailed breakdown of how much time you're spending on different apps. Use these tools to set up daily limits, and you'll get notifications when you're close to hitting your max for the day. Trust me, those reminders can be quite the wake-up call!

Moreover, parents and guardians can play an important role by setting consistent rules and modeling good behavior. Having family tech-free zones, like during dinner or before bedtime, can make a big difference. The goal here isn't to go cold turkey but to find a sustainable way to manage your screen use—leaving room for other important activities that contribute to overall well-being.

Detrimental Effects of Overexposure

Now, let's talk about what happens when we don't manage our screen time effectively. Picture this: It's midnight, you've been scrolling through TikTok for hours, and suddenly you realize your eyes feel like they've been fried. If this sounds familiar, you're not alone.

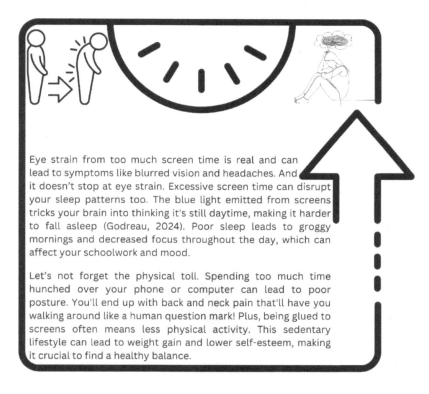

Eye strain from too much screen time is real and can lead to symptoms like blurred vision and headaches. And it doesn't stop at eye strain. Excessive screen time can disrupt your sleep patterns too. The blue light emitted from screens tricks your brain into thinking it's still daytime, making it harder to fall asleep (Godreau, 2024). Poor sleep leads to groggy mornings and decreased focus throughout the day, which can affect your schoolwork and mood.

Let's not forget the physical toll. Spending too much time hunched over your phone or computer can lead to poor posture. You'll end up with back and neck pain that'll have you walking around like a human question mark! Plus, being glued to screens often means less physical activity. This sedentary lifestyle can lead to weight gain and lower self-esteem, making it crucial to find a healthy balance.

Healthy Alternatives

Alright, so if you're limiting screen time, what's the game plan for filling in the gaps? Healthy alternatives are the way to go. Think about diving into activities that get you moving and socializing. For instance, how about picking up a new hobby like drawing, playing a musical instrument, or even cooking?

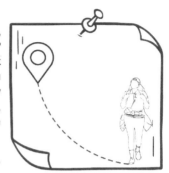

If you're someone who loves the outdoors, consider hiking, biking, or playing sports with friends. Physical activities aren't just good for your body; they also release those feel-good endorphins that boost your mood and self-esteem. Got a dog? Perfect! They'll love those extra walks, and it's a great excuse to get outside. Social activities are another excellent alternative. Nothing beats hanging out with friends face-to-face. Plan a movie night,

organize a board game session, or just catch up over a cup of coffee.

Real-world interactions are far more enriching than endless scrolling through social media feeds. The key is to find something that excites you, so you're less tempted to reach for your phone.

Lastly, don't underestimate the power of quiet activities like reading a book or writing in a journal. These can be very rewarding and offer a nice break from the digital world. Start a small garden, paint your room, or learn to bake—a delicious reward awaits you!

Mindfulness and Reflection

To round things off, let's delve into mindfulness and reflection. Ever heard the mantra "be present"? Mindfulness practices can help you become more aware of how you're spending your time and why.

One way to incorporate mindfulness is through journaling. Keep a diary where you jot down your digital habits. Reflect on questions like, "How did I feel after spending X amount of time on social media?" or "What could I have done instead of binge-watching that show?" This can provide valuable insights and help you adjust your habits over time.

Another effective practice is mindful breathing or meditation. Even just five minutes a day can make a huge difference. Apps like Headspace or Calm offer guided meditations specifically designed to help improve focus and reduce stress. You might find that the urge to check your phone every few minutes diminishes as you grow more comfortable with just being present in the moment.

Discussing your digital habits with friends or family can also be illuminating. You might discover common struggles and share strategies for improvement. It's reassuring to know you're not alone in this digital dance.

Recognizing and Avoiding Phishing Scams

Phishing is like a digital version of trick-or-treat, but with much scarier consequences than finding raisins in your candy bag. Essentially, phishing is a scamming technique where cybercriminals try to steal personal information by pretending to be trustworthy entities. They might disguise themselves as your bank, a social media site, or even your favorite online store. Understanding phishing is your first armor against these sneaky tricks.

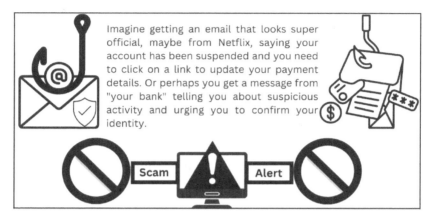

Imagine getting an email that looks super official, maybe from Netflix, saying your account has been suspended and you need to click on a link to update your payment details. Or perhaps you get a message from "your bank" telling you about suspicious activity and urging you to confirm your identity.

Scam Alert

These are classic examples of phishing attempts. The emails and messages often look legitimate and can have logos, official-looking signatures, and even fake websites designed to mimic the real thing.

One thing that sets off alarm bells about phishing attempts is their poor grammar and spelling errors. It's like the scammers flunked English class and still decided to go ahead and write their email scams anyway. If you see an email that's riddled with typos, especially if it's supposed to be from a professional entity, be very cautious. Real businesses usually hire people who can spell properly.

Another red flag is a sense of urgency. Scammers want you to act before you think. They'll tell you your account will be closed, you'll lose access to funds, or some other dire consequence if you don't click on their link ASAP. Take a deep breath and remember: Legitimate companies rarely ask for immediate action through unsolicited emails or messages.

Suspicious links are another giveaway. These links might look normal at first glance, but if you hover your cursor over them without clicking, you'll often see the true destination, which is usually a shady web address. It's like when someone offers you candy, but you peek and see they've got a handful of rocks instead. Just don't click on it.

When it comes to safe browsing practices, always make sure the websites you visit are legitimate. Look for HTTPS in the web address bar rather than just HTTP – that extra 'S' means the site is secure. Be wary of misspelled URLs or sites that look slightly off. It's like spotting a knockoff handbag; it might look similar at first, but a closer inspection shows it's not the real deal.

Using trusted security software is also crucial. This software can help block malicious websites and alert you to potential threats. Think of it as having a digital bodyguard who's always on the lookout for sketchy characters. Make sure your software is up to date so it's ready to fend off the latest scams.

Now, let's talk about multi-factor authentication (MFA), which is like adding an extra deadbolt to your front door. MFA requires two or more verification steps to log into your accounts. These might include something you know, like a password, and something you have, like a texted code or an app-generated token. It makes it way harder for scammers to get in, even if they have your password. So, whenever possible, enable MFA on all your accounts (Federal Trade Commission, 2022).

Backing up your data regularly is another safe browsing practice. Whether it's on an external hard drive or in the cloud, having a backup ensures that even if your device gets compromised, your important information remains safe and sound. It's like having an emergency supply kit at the ready.

If you suspect you've encountered a phishing attempt, don't panic. First, report the phishing attempt. Forward phishing emails to the Anti-Phishing Working Group at reportphishing@apwg.org, and send phishing texts to SPAM (7726). Reporting these attempts helps authorities track down and tackle cybercriminals (Federal Trade Commission, 2022).

Next, inform trusted adults or relevant authorities. If it's related to work or school accounts, notify your IT department. It's like sounding the alarm so everyone can take necessary precautions. If you've accidentally shared sensitive information, change your passwords immediately and ensure you use unique ones for different accounts. You might even want to check out a password manager to keep everything organized securely.

In cases where sensitive financial information, like credit card numbers, has been shared, contact your bank or credit card company right away to alert them about potential fraud. They can help monitor your accounts for suspicious activity. Also, keeping a close eye on your statements for any unexpected transactions is a good idea.

Lastly, if the phishing attack leads to identity theft or significant financial loss, don't hesitate to involve local law enforcement. They can investigate and possibly catch the culprits. Plus, having a record of the incident can be helpful for insurance claims or other legal actions.

Responding to Cyberbullying Appropriately

Recognizing Cyberbullying Signs

Alright, let's dive into the world of cyberbullying. First things first, what exactly is cyber bullying? Simply put, it's bullying that takes place over digital devices like phones, computers, and tablets. It can happen through SMS, Text, and apps, or online in social media, forums, or gaming where people can view, participate in, or share content. Now, cyberbullying comes in many forms. It could be mean text messages or emails, rumors sent by email or posted on social networking sites, and embarrassing pictures, videos, websites, or fake profiles.

Recognizing the signs of cyberbullying in yourself can be key to dealing with it effectively. Do you find yourself using your devices a lot more or a lot less than usual? That change in screen time could be a red flag. Notice your emotional reactions: if you often laugh, get angry, or feel upset over something you see on your device, it's important to pay attention. You might also catch yourself hiding your screen when others are around or shutting down your social media accounts, only to quickly create new ones. These could all be signs that something isn't right.

Steps to Take if You're Being Bullied

So, what should you do if you're being bullied? Here's a game plan to tackle this head-on. First off, document the incidents. Keep a record of every nasty message, screenshot mean posts, and save any evidence you can gather. This will be super helpful if you need to report the bullying later on. Next, block the bully. Most social media platforms allow you to block users who are bothering you. Use this feature to keep them from contacting you again.

Speaking of reporting, most platforms and schools have processes for reporting cyber bullying. Don't hesitate to tell someone about it. Trusted adults, teachers, or even friends can provide support and advice. And don't forget about the power of self-care. Sometimes just taking a break from your device can help reduce stress and give you a moment to breathe.

How to Support Others

Now, it's not just about protecting yourself—you can be a hero for others too. If you see someone else being bullied, there are ways to step in and help. You can start by being an ally. Stand up for your friends online by expressing your support both privately and publicly. Send them a kind message, or comment positively to counteract the negativity they're facing.

Initiating conversations can also make a big difference. Sometimes just asking if they're okay and letting them know you're there for them can be incredibly powerful. And don't forget to report incidents. Whether it's to a teacher, a parent, or even directly to the social media platform, reporting can help stop the bully in their tracks.

Building a Positive Online Community

To create a safe digital environment, it's crucial to promote positivity and kindness online. Encourage respectful interactions and stand firm against any form of bullying. Simple acts like giving compliments, sharing positive posts, or creating uplifting content can set the tone for a kinder, gentler internet.

You can also start initiatives or join groups dedicated to spreading good vibes online. Be mindful of what you post and always think before hitting "send." Would your words hurt someone? If yes, maybe reconsider posting them. Remember, creating a positive space starts with individual actions, and each person has the power to make the internet a better place.

Navigating the digital world confidently involves a mix of smart strategies and tools. This chapter has shown you how to create strong passwords, use password managers, and enable two-factor authentication to keep your online life safe from hackers. Remember, setting up alerts and regularly checking your privacy settings can help you catch any suspicious activity early on. By adopting these practices, you'll build a solid defense against cyber threats.

But it's not just about staying secure; it's also about being mindful and proactive in your online habits. Keeping track of your screen time, recognizing phishing scams, and knowing how to respond to cyberbullying are crucial steps. Balancing digital life with offline activities and supporting others in the online community makes your overall experience not only safer but also more enjoyable. Keep these tips in mind, and you'll be well-equipped to handle the digital landscape like a pro!

CHAPTER 12

PLANNING FOR THE FUTURE

Planning for the Future

oes planning for the future feel overwhelming? What if I told you it's actually an exciting adventure full of possibilities? Whether you're envisioning a career that aligns with your wildest passions or just trying to figure out the next step after high school, there's so much to explore. The goal is to turn those dreams into actionable goals, equipping you with the tools and strategies to navigate your academic and professional journey. Remember, it's not about having all the answers right now—it's about laying the groundwork for endless opportunities tomorrow.

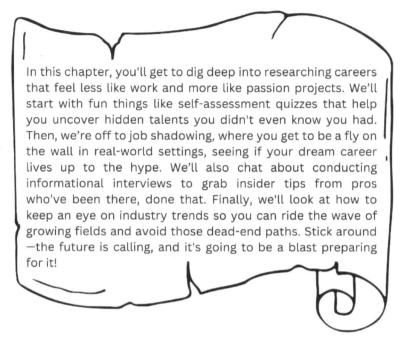

In this chapter, you'll get to dig deep into researching careers that feel less like work and more like passion projects. We'll start with fun things like self-assessment quizzes that help you uncover hidden talents you didn't even know you had. Then, we're off to job shadowing, where you get to be a fly on the wall in real-world settings, seeing if your dream career lives up to the hype. We'll also chat about conducting informational interviews to grab insider tips from pros who've been there, done that. Finally, we'll look at how to keep an eye on industry trends so you can ride the wave of growing fields and avoid those dead-end paths. Stick around —the future is calling, and it's going to be a blast preparing for it!

Researching Possible Careers Based on Interests

Exploring career options that align with your passions and interests is crucial for laying a solid foundation for future success. Imagine waking up every day excited to go to work because you genuinely love what you do. This isn't just a fantasy; it's achievable by taking the right steps to identify and pursue careers that resonate with you.

First things first, let's talk about self-assessment tools like quizzes and surveys. These might sound trivial, but they can be incredibly enlightening. There are various career assessment quizzes designed to help pinpoint your interests and strengths. Think of these quizzes as a fun way to better understand yourself. They'll often ask about your hobbies, preferences in working environments, whether you prefer working alone or in teams, and more. Based on your responses, they suggest career paths that are well-suited to your personality type. For instance, if you love solving problems and enjoy detailed work, a quiz might suggest careers like engineering or data analysis. Utilizing these self-assessment tools can streamline your focus towards careers you're likely to enjoy and excel in.

Now, let's dive into job shadowing. Job shadowing is an absolute game-changer when it comes to career exploration. Picture this: spending a day with a professional in a field you're interested in. You get to see firsthand what their job entails—everything from the mundane tasks to the exciting projects. This experience can provide a clearer picture of whether a particular career fits your expectations. For example, if you're considering a career in medicine, shadowing a doctor will expose you to the realities of patient care, administrative duties, and the high-energy environment of a hospital. Job shadowing not only gives you insights into daily responsibilities but also helps you decide if a career is truly right for you.

Following on, conducting informational interviews is another excellent strategy for gaining career insights. An informational interview involves having a one-on-one conversation with someone who works in a field you're interested in. You get the chance to ask questions about their day-to-day responsibilities, challenges they face, and what they enjoy most about their job. Imagine sitting down with a graphic designer and learning about the creative process behind designing a brand's logo, the software they use, and the kind of clients they work with. Such interviews can demystify career paths and reveal aspects you might not have considered. Plus, it's a great way to build your network and potentially find mentors who can guide you along your career journey.

Another critical aspect of planning for the future is understanding job market trends. You might have a passion for something, but it's equally important to know if that passion aligns with growing industries. Staying informed about industry growth can help you identify viable career options that offer stability and opportunities for advancement. For instance, careers in technology and healthcare are rapidly expanding, providing numerous job openings and chances for growth. Conversely, some fields might be shrinking, making jobs harder to come by. Researching job market trends involves keeping an eye on reports and forecasts about which professions are expected to grow. This ensures that you're not only pursuing your passions but also making smart career choices that promise a bright future.

Combining these strategies provides a comprehensive approach to exploring career options. Start with self-assessment tools to discover where your interests lie. Follow up with job shadowing to gain real-world insights into those careers. Conduct informational interviews to deepen your understanding and clarify any uncertainties. Finally, stay informed about industry trends to ensure you're moving towards a promising and stable career.

The beauty of this holistic approach is that it empowers you to make informed decisions about your future. Rather than stumbling upon a career by chance, you're actively shaping your path based on thorough exploration and genuine interest. This proactive approach not only boosts your confidence but also enhances your readiness for the challenges and opportunities that lie ahead.

So, imagine kicking off this journey with a simple career quiz. You spend 15 minutes answering questions about your likes and dislikes. Voila! You've got a list of potential careers that match your personality. Next, you reach out to your school counselor to set up a job shadowing day with someone in one of those careers. Maybe you spend a day at a local law firm, following a lawyer around and soaking in all the legal jargon and courtroom drama. Intrigued, you decide to dig deeper. You find a lawyer willing to chat over a cup of coffee, sharing candid insights about the highs and lows of their career. Armed with this knowledge, you start researching labor statistics and discover that demand for lawyers is stable. Not only do you now know that being a lawyer fascinates you, but you've also confirmed it's a viable career option.

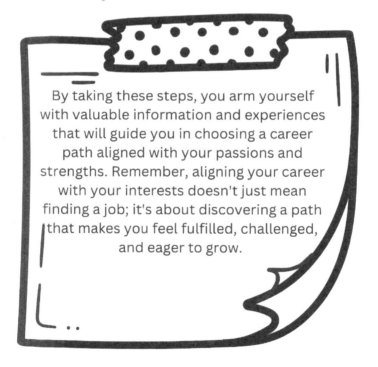

By taking these steps, you arm yourself with valuable information and experiences that will guide you in choosing a career path aligned with your passions and strengths. Remember, aligning your career with your interests doesn't just mean finding a job; it's about discovering a path that makes you feel fulfilled, challenged, and eager to grow.

Preparing for College or Trade School Applications

Navigating the college or trade school application process can feel like an epic journey. But fear not! With a little planning and some helpful strategies, you can tackle this beast head-on and emerge victorious. Here's a structured approach to help you prepare your applications confidently.

First things first, you've got to do your homework – and I don't mean algebra. Researching specific school criteria is crucial if you want to create a tailored application strategy. Every school has its quirks and unique requirements, so it's vital to understand what each one expects from applicants. Whether it's certain GPA thresholds, extracurricular activities, or specific essay topics, knowing these details in advance lets you align your profile with their preferences. For example, some schools place a heavy emphasis on volunteer work, while others might prioritize leadership roles or artistic talent. Get cozy with the websites of the colleges or trade schools you're interested in. This will be your treasure map, guiding you through the maze of requirements and deadlines. Imagine you're Sherlock Holmes, but instead of solving crimes, you're uncovering the secrets to getting into your dream school.

Speaking of deadlines, organizing timelines effectively will keep the whole process manageable and far less terrifying. Start early and set deadlines for completing different components of your application well before the actual due date. We're talking essays, letters of recommendation, test scores, and all those pesky forms. Set internal deadlines a few weeks ahead just to be safe. Mark these dates on your calendar or use a spreadsheet – whatever keeps you on track.

Being proactive about deadlines relieves stress and gives you that sweet cushion of time in case something goes awry. Trust me, nothing is worse than realizing you need one more recommendation letter at the last minute. (<i>College Application Advice: Tips to Streamline the Process – BigFuture</i>, n.d.)

Now, let's talk letters of recommendation. Choosing the right people to vouch for your abilities is like picking your dream team. These individuals should know you well enough to provide strong endorsements of your skills and character. Teachers, coaches, or supervisors who have seen you in action and can speak to your strengths are ideal candidates. Don't just go for the big names; opt for those who genuinely know and appreciate your work. And remember to ask them well in advance to avoid any last-minute scrambles. It's also helpful to provide them with a summary of your achievements and a gentle reminder of any deadlines they need to meet. This makes it easier for them to write a thoughtful and timely letter. The goal is to make it as easy as possible for your recommenders to sing your praises.

Next up is crafting a compelling personal statement. This is your chance to shine and give the admissions committee a glimpse of who you really are beyond grades and test scores. Start by brainstorming experiences that have shaped you and reflect on how they tie into your goals and values. Maybe it was that summer volunteering at a local animal shelter that sparked your passion for veterinary science, or perhaps leading your debate team taught you invaluable leadership skills. Whatever your stories are, make sure they highlight your unique journey and voice. Authenticity is key here.

Admissions officers read countless essays, so a genuine, heartfelt narrative stands out. (<i>What Looks Good on College Applications?</i>, n.d.)

Avoid generic statements and clichés. Instead, focus on specific moments that had a significant impact on your life. What lessons did you learn? How did these experiences shape your aspirations? A good way to start your essay is with a captivating anecdote that draws the reader in. Then, weave in reflections and insights that show personal growth and resilience. Oh, and did I mention proofreading? Yes, a bazillion times yes. Nothing sours an excellent essay like typos and grammatical errors. Have a teacher, parent, or friend review your essay for clarity and correctness.

Developing a Compelling Resume and Cover Letter

Creating a resume and cover letter that make you stand out can seem overwhelming at first, but we're here to break it down into manageable steps. Think of your resume and cover letter as your first impression in the professional world—they should showcase your unique skills and experiences clearly and confidently.

Components of a Stellar Resume

A great resume starts with its structure. The essential sections include contact information, a resume summary or objective, work experience, education, and skills. Let's dive into each of these:

1. **Contact Information**: This is the simplest part—your name, phone number, email address, and LinkedIn profile (if you have one). Make sure this information is at the very top so employers can easily reach out if they're interested.

2. **Resume Summary or Objective**: If you're just starting out, an objective statement is perfect. It briefly outlines your career goals and what you aim to achieve. For those with more experience, a resume summary might be more fitting. It highlights your key achievements and skills using active language.

3. **Work Experience**: List your jobs in reverse-chronological order, starting with the most recent. Include the company name, your job title, and the dates you worked there. Describe your responsibilities and accomplishments using bullet points. This makes it easy for employers to scan through quickly.

4. **Education**: Here, list your high school, any college credit courses, and other educational programs. Include relevant coursework that demonstrates your knowledge base.

5. **Skills**: Divide this section into two parts—hard skills and soft skills. Hard skills are technical abilities like proficiency in Microsoft Office or coding languages. Soft skills are interpersonal traits like communication or teamwork. Tailor your skills to match the job description you're applying for (Indeed Editorial Team, 2023).

6. **Formatting**: Keep your resume clean and simple. Use a readable font like Arial or Times New Roman, and don't go overboard with colors. Consistent formatting helps employers focus on the content.

Powerful Action Verbs

Ever feel like your resume sounds a bit lifeless? Spruce it up with strong action verbs. Instead of saying "Responsible for managing," say "Managed." Instead of "Was in charge of," use "Led." Action verbs lend strength to your descriptions and demonstrate impact. Some fantastic verbs include "developed," "initiated," "designed," and "achieved."

Imagine you volunteered at a local shelter and organized donation drives. Instead of "Helped organize donation drives," say "Organized and led donation drives, increasing community donations by 30%." Sounds way cooler, right?

Writing an Engaging Cover Letter

Your cover letter is your chance to speak directly to the employer or admissions officer. It's where you show your personality and explain why you're the best fit for the role or program. Here's a straightforward formula:

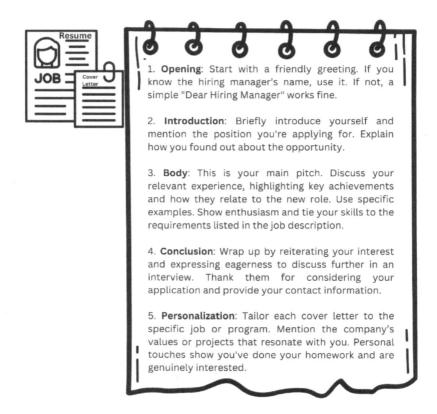

Utilizing Online Resources

The internet is your best friend when it comes to building resumes and cover letters. Websites like Indeed, LinkedIn, and even YouTube offer free templates, tutorials, and tips. Career centers often provide excellent resources too (Resume & Cover Letter Guide | Community College of Philadelphia, 2024).

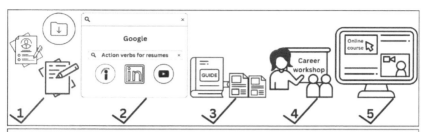

1. **Templates and Samples**: Many sites offer downloadable templates. Choose one that fits your style but remember to personalize it. Templates are just starting points.

2. **Action Verb Lists**: Struggling to find the right words? Google "action verbs for resumes" and you'll get numerous lists to choose from.

3. **Step-by-Step Guides**: Find guides that walk you through the process of writing each section of your resume and cover letter. They usually include examples and pro tips.

4. **Career Services**: Utilize services provided by your school or local community centers. Many offer workshops, one-on-one guidance, and resume reviews.

5. **Online Courses**: Platforms like Coursera or Skillshare offer courses on resume writing and job hunting. These can provide in-depth insights and advanced tips.

Real-Life Examples

It helps to see these tips in action, so let's take a look at an example for both a resume and a cover letter.

Sample Resume Section 1:

Jane Doe

CONTACT

 (123) 456-7890

 janedoe@example.com

 123 Main St, Hometown, USA

EXPERIENCE

June 2020–August 2021

Volunteer, Local Animal Shelter
Hometown, USA

- Organized fundraising drives, increasing donations by 30%
- Assisted in daily care and feeding of animals
- Coordinated volunteer schedules

OBJECTIVE

High school graduate with a passion for environmental science seeking an internship at Green Earth Co. to gain practical experience and contribute to sustainability efforts.

SKILLS

- Proficient in Microsoft Word and Excel
- Strong communication and organizational skills
- Basic knowledge of Photoshop

EDUCATION

- June 2021
- Hometown High School Graduated
- Relevant Coursework: AP Environmental Science, Biology, Chemistry

Sample Resume Section 2:

Jane Doe

OBJECTIVE

High school graduate with a passion for environmental science seeking an internship at Green Earth Co. to gain practical experience and contribute to sustainability efforts.

EDUCATION

- June 2021
  Hometown High School
- Graduated
  Relevant Coursework: AP
- Environmental Science, Biology, Chemistry

CONTACT

 (123) 456-7890

 janedoe@example.com

 123 Main St, Hometown, USA

SKILLS

- Proficient in Microsoft Word and Excel
- Strong communication and organizational skills
- Basic knowledge of Photoshop

EXPERIENCE

June 2020–August 2021

Volunteer, Local Animal Shelter Hometown, USA

- Organized fundraising drives, increasing donations by 30%
- Assisted in daily care and feeding of animals
- Coordinated volunteer schedules

Sample Cover Letter:

JANE DOE

(123) 456-7890
janedoe@example.com
123 Main St, Hometown, USA

(The name of the hiring manager here)   Date:__/__/___
Hiring Manager, Green Earth Co.
123 Anywhere St., Any City

Dear Hiring Manager,

I'm excited to apply for the internship position at Green Earth Co. I recently graduated from Hometown High School where my interest in environmental science grew through various projects and volunteer work. I'm passionate about sustainability and eager to bring my enthusiasm and skills to your team.

During my time volunteering at the local animal shelter, I organized several successful fundraising drives, which increased our donations by 30%. This experience taught me the importance of community involvement and effective communication. I believe these skills will be valuable in supporting your company's initiatives.

I am particularly drawn to Green Earth Co.'s mission to promote sustainable living and would love the opportunity to contribute to your projects. Thank you for considering my application. I look forward to the possibility of discussing how my background, skills, and ambitions align with your needs.

Best regards,

Jane Doe

Practicing Interview Skills and Etiquette

One of the best ways to prepare for an interview is by familiarizing yourself with common interview questions. You know, questions like, "Tell me about yourself," or "What are your strengths and weaknesses?" These questions might seem straightforward, but they often trip people up because they require thoughtful and honest responses. The trick is to think about your answers beforehand, jot down some bullet points, and practice them until they feel natural. This not only helps you answer more confidently but also reduces those pre-interview jitters. (Herrity, 2017)

Next up, participating in mock interviews can be a game-changer. Imagine you're an actress preparing for a big role—practice makes perfect, right? The same goes for interviews. Get a friend, family member, or even a teacher to play the interviewer. Go through the entire process, from greeting them with a firm handshake to answering questions and asking some of your own. This simulation helps you get used to the format and timing of real interviews, making you more comfortable when the actual day arrives.

Speaking of comfort, let's talk about appropriate behaviors and attire. It's essential to show respect for the interview process and align with the organization's culture. For instance, if you're interviewing at a tech startup where everyone wears jeans and hoodies, you might opt for business-casual attire. On the other hand, if it's a corporate setting, go for a more formal look—think blazers, dress pants, or a knee-length skirt. Always check your clothes for any pet hair, stains, or wrinkles before you leave the house. A neat appearance shows that you care about the opportunity and have made an effort to present yourself well. (Heine, 2023)

Now, let's move on to non-verbal cues, which are just as important as what you say during an interview. Confident body language can significantly influence how interviewers perceive you. Sit up straight, make eye contact, and don't forget to smile. These gestures project confidence and approachability.

Practice these non-verbal cues in front of a mirror or record yourself to see how you come across. Also, avoid fidgeting with your hands or feet; it can be distracting and give off the impression that you're nervous or unprepared.

For example, imagine you're asked a challenging question about a past failure. Instead of slouching and mumbling your way through the response, sit up straight, take a deep breath, and maintain eye contact. Use your hands to emphasize key points, but keep your movements controlled and purposeful. This kind of body language not only makes you appear more confident but also helps you feel more in control of the situation.

Understanding professional etiquette is another critical aspect. When you're in an interview, you're being evaluated not just on your answers, but on your overall demeanor. It starts the moment you walk into the building. Greet everyone you meet with a smile and a polite hello, whether it's the receptionist or the actual interviewer. This shows that you're respectful and considerate, traits that any employer would value. (Herrity, 2017)

When it comes to answering questions, remember to be concise and focused. Rambling on can make you appear unfocused and unprepared. Stick to the STAR method—Situation, Task, Action, Result—when framing your answers. This helps you provide structured and complete responses without going off on tangents. For instance, if you're asked about a time you solved a problem, start by briefly explaining the situation, what task was at hand, the actions you took to address it, and finally, the positive result that came out of it. This method keeps your answers clear and impactful.

After you've tackled the questions, you'll usually get a chance to ask some of your own. This is your opportunity to show that you're genuinely interested in the role and the company. Prepare a few smart questions in advance, such as, "Can you describe the team I'll be working with?" or "What are the biggest challenges facing the company right now?" This not only demonstrates your enthusiasm but also gives you valuable insights into whether the job is the right fit for you. (Herrity, 2017)

Another useful tip is to prepare a list of references before the interview. Sometimes, interviewers may ask for references on the spot, and having a list ready can save you from scrambling at the last minute. Choose people who can vouch for your skills and character, like a former teacher or a supervisor from a part-time job. Make sure to ask for their permission before listing them as references, and let them know they might be contacted soon.

On the day of the interview, plan to arrive 10 to 15 minutes early. This shows punctuality and respect for the interviewer's time. Use those extra minutes to observe the workplace dynamics. Notice how employees interact with each other and what kind of environment it seems to be. These observations can give you additional talking points during the interview and help you decide if the company's culture aligns with your values.

Finally, remember the importance of first impressions. Shine your shoes, brush or style your hair, and ensure your nails are clean. Check your clothes for any last-minute issues like stains or loose threads. And most importantly, don't forget to smile. A genuine smile can set a positive tone for the entire interview, making you seem approachable and enthusiastic.

Alright, ladies, we've covered a lot in this chapter about gearing up for your future. From figuring out your dream job through fun quizzes and eye-opening job shadowing experiences to having those all-important informational interviews with professionals in fields you're curious about, you're now armed with tools to navigate your post-high school path like a pro. And let's not forget the importance of keeping an eye on job market trends to make sure your passion aligns with industries that offer stability and growth.

So, what's the takeaway? It's all about taking charge of your future with confidence and curiosity. By using these strategies, you'll be able to make informed decisions that lead to a fulfilling career and academic journey. Remember, it's not just about landing a job; it's about finding something that excites you and keeps you motivated every day. So get out there, explore, ask questions, and most importantly, have fun with it! You're crafting a future that's uniquely yours—now go make it amazing!

CONCLUSION

Wow, we've reached the end of our epic journey together! Wherever you are reading this, whether it's snuggled up in your favorite cozy corner or plopped down on the school bus, I want you to take a big, deep breath and pat yourself on the back. We've crammed in so many crucial life skills that I'm pretty sure we could start a superhero team right now – "The Teenage Girl Avengers" has a nice ring to it, don't you think?

Let's hit the rewind button for a sec and recap what we've tackled along the way. We went from boosting self-esteem (yes, you're all unique unicorns) to nailing personal hygiene (who knew being fresh and fabulous was so important?). Then, we took a culinary detour into cooking— because let's face it, mastering the art of making a killer grilled cheese is basically a life requirement. Oh, and let's not forget about finances – budgeting might sound super boring, but knowing how to handle your money is basically a magic trick for future success. Each one of these skills is like a shiny puzzle piece fitting perfectly into the grand picture of you becoming an independent, self-confident, and downright amazing young woman.

But here's the real kicker: Learning doesn't stop just because we're flipping the last page of this book. Nope, life is one long rollercoaster of new challenges and hilarious mistakes. So, keep that curiosity alive! If you ever find yourself staring at yet another YouTube tutorial trying to figure out how to change a flat tire, remember that each little snippet of knowledge you pick up is another step towards becoming even more awesome. Practice makes perfect, and before you know it, you'll be impressing everyone with your newfound talents. Even if you're not perfect right away—embrace those cringe-worthy moments and learn from them. They're part of your growth story, too!

Speaking of growth, have you thought about how much you've already achieved? Think back to when you first picked up this book. Maybe you were nervous about managing stress or unsure about how to start a conversation with someone new. But look at you now! Sure, you may not have transformed into some mythical creature who can do everything flawlessly overnight, but the small steps count. Have you tried a new recipe lately? Or maybe you successfully saved up for something you really wanted without blowing all your cash on impulse buys (yay, you!). Recognizing these little victories is key. They show just how far you've come on this wild ride called life, building up your confidence bit by bit.

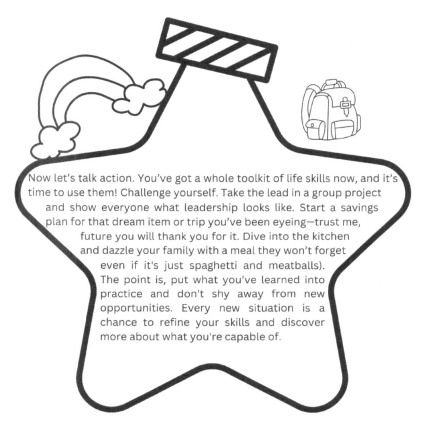

Now let's talk action. You've got a whole toolkit of life skills now, and it's time to use them! Challenge yourself. Take the lead in a group project and show everyone what leadership looks like. Start a savings plan for that dream item or trip you've been eyeing—trust me, future you will thank you for it. Dive into the kitchen and dazzle your family with a meal they won't forget even if it's just spaghetti and meatballs). The point is, put what you've learned into practice and don't shy away from new opportunities. Every new situation is a chance to refine your skills and discover more about what you're capable of.

And hey, guess what? The future is beaming, practically shouting at you to jump in and make your mark. With the skills and confidence you've gained, there's no stopping you. Embrace every moment, laugh off the goof-ups, and keep pushing forward. Whether you're dreaming of starting your own business, traveling the world, or simply being the best version of yourself, know that you've got the tools to make it happen.

So here we are, at the close of our book but nowhere near the end of your adventure. Armed with your newfound knowledge and skills, you are ready to conquer whatever comes next. Remember, you're a rockstar in the making.

Go out there and shine like the brilliant, capable, and fabulous young woman you are.

And if you ever need a refresher, just flip back through these pages — I'm always here, cheering you on.

Keep learning, keep growing, and most importantly, keep being you. Because you've totally got this. Now go forth, live boldly, and make waves. The world better watch out, because you're just getting started!

RESOURCES AND FURTHER READING

1. Recommended Books

- **Life Skills and Personal Development:**
  - "The 7 Habits of Highly Effective Teens" by Sean Covey
  - "How to Win Friends and Influence People for Teen Girls" by Donna Dale Carnegie
  - "Grit for Girls: 10 Keys to Building Confidence & Achieving Greatness" by Angela Duckworth

- **Health and Wellbeing:**
  - "The Teen Girl's Survival Guide: Ten Tips for Making Friends, Avoiding Drama, and Coping with Social Stress" by Lucie Hemmen
  - "The Self-Esteem Workbook for Teens" by Lisa M. Schab
  - "The Body Book for Younger Girls" by Dr. Cara Natterson

- **Cooking and Nutrition:**
  - o "Teens Cook: How to Cook What You Want to Eat" by Megan Carle and Jill Carle
  - o "The Super Easy Teen Baking Cookbook" by Cora Pineda
- **Financial Literacy:**
  - o "I Want More Pizza: Real World Money Skills for High School, College, and Beyond" by Steve Burkholder
  - o "Smart Money Smart Kids: Raising the Next Generation to Win with Money" by Dave Ramsey and Rachel Cruze

2. Websites and Online Resources

- **Life Skills and Personal Growth:**
  - o **MindTools:** www.mindtools.comOffers practical resources on time management, communication skills, and decision-making.
  - o **Teen Health & Wellness:** www.teenhealthandwellness.comA comprehensive resource on mental health, physical health, and personal safety.
  - o **Girls Leadership:** www.girlsleadership.orgProvides online courses, workshops, and resources focused on leadership and empowerment for girls.
- **Cooking and DIY Projects:**
  - o **AllRecipes:** www.allrecipes.comOffers a variety of recipes with step-by-step instructions and videos.

- o **DIY Network:** www.diynetwork.comA website with a wide range of DIY projects for beginners and experts alike.

- **Financial Literacy:**
  - o **MoneySense:** www.mymoneysense.comOffers tools and tips for teens on managing money, budgeting, and saving.
  - o **The Mint:** www.themint.orgProvides interactive activities and lessons on earning, saving, spending, and borrowing.

- **Digital Skills and Safety:**
  - o **Common Sense Media:** www.commonsensemedia.orgProvides reviews and resources for navigating digital content responsibly.
  - o **Stay Safe Online:** www.staysafeonline.orgOffers tips and advice on online privacy and cybersecurity for teens.

3. Apps for Daily Life

- **Time Management and Productivity:**
  - o **Trello:** A task management app to help organize projects and to-do lists. www.trello.com
  - o **Forest:** A focus and time management app that helps users stay away from their phones. www.forestapp.cc

- **Health and Wellness:**
  - o **Headspace:** A meditation and mindfulness app designed to reduce stress and improve focus. www.headspace.com

- o   **MyFitnessPal:** A nutrition and fitness tracker to help maintain healthy eating habits. www.myfitnesspal.com

- **Financial Management:**

  - o   **Mint:** A personal finance app that helps with budgeting, tracking expenses, and managing money. www.mint.com

  - o   **YNAB (You Need A Budget):** A budgeting app that teaches budgeting techniques to help save money. www.ynab.com

4. Helplines and Support Organizations

- **Mental Health:**

  - o   **National Suicide Prevention Lifeline:** 1-800-273-TALK (8255) - Confidential support for those in distress.

  - o   **Crisis Text Line:** Text HOME to 741741 for free, 24/7 crisis support.

- **General Support:**

  - o   **Teen Line:** Call 310-855-4673 or text "TEEN" to 839863 - A helpline for teens to talk about any issues they are facing.

  - o   **Girls Inc.:** Provides support and advocacy for young girls through educational programs and resources. www.girlsinc.org

5. Additional Skills to Explore and Learn

- **Creative Skills:**
  - Explore arts and crafts through online tutorials and local workshops.
  - Join clubs or online communities focused on writing, drawing, or other creative interests.

- **Leadership and Community Involvement:**
  - Volunteer at local organizations to build leadership skills and give back to the community.
  - Join school clubs or start a new club focused on a cause or interest area.

REFERENCES

1. 10 Essential Self-Care Practices. (2023, July 6). *Wellness Road Psychology.* https://www.wellnessroadpsychology.com/10-essential-self-care-practices/

2. 10 Tips for Balancing Academics and Social Life: A Guide for PhD Students - ARU. (n.d.). Www.aru.ac.uk. https://www.aru.ac.uk/blogs/10-tips-for-balancing-academics-and-social-life

3. 100 Smart Goal Examples: Plus Printable PDF resources. (n.d.). *Wise Goals.* https://www.wisegoals.com/smart-goal-examples.html

4. 10+ Fun Career Exploration Activities: Broadening Horizons and Inspiring Futures. (n.d.). *Educationadvanced.com.* https://educationadvanced.com/blog/fun-career-exploration-activities

5. A Guide to Practicing Self-Care with Mindfulness. (2020, December 18). *Mindful.* https://www.mindful.org/a-guide-to-practicing-self-care-with-mindfulness/

6. Bell, A. (2024, March 25). What are the 5 purposes of budgeting? *Investopedia.* https://www.investopedia.com/financial-edge/1109/6-reasons-why-you-need-a-budget.aspx

7. Bennett, R. (2023, June 20). 5 Ways To Avoid Impulse Buying. *Bankrate.* https://www.bankrate.com/banking/savings/ways-to-avoid-impulse-buying/

8. CISA. (2023). Multi-Factor Authentication | CISA. Www.cisa.gov. https://www.cisa.gov/mfa

9. Cleveland Clinic. (2024, May 15). What Is Stress? *Cleveland Clinic.* https://my.clevelandclinic.org/health/diseases/11874-stress

10. College Application Advice: Tips to Streamline the Process – BigFuture. (n.d.). *Bigfuture.collegeboard.org.* https://bigfuture.collegeboard.org/plan-for-college/apply-to-college/application-process/tips-for-preparing-your-college-application

11. Corporation, L. (2015, March 8). Basic Safety Rules for Hand Tools (originally from www.teched101.com). *Lowell Corporation.* https://lowellcorp.com/basic-safety-rules-for-hand-tools-originally-from-www-teched101-com/

12. Cote, C. (2022, July 6). Why Is Budgeting Important in Business? 5 Reasons. *Harvard Business School Online.* https://online.hbs.edu/blog/post/importance-of-budgeting-in-business

13. Coursera. (2024, February 1). What Is Effective Communication? Skills for Work, School, and Life. *Coursera.* https://www.coursera.org/articles/communication-effectiveness

14. Cruze, R. (2024, June 28). Impulse Buying: What It Is and How to Stop. *Ramsey Solutions.* https://www.ramseysolutions.com/budgeting/stop-impulse-buys?srsltid=AfmBOooimJ0_se1O3w4Bbe9wq0ja_BJ5sbmakCgA-p0Mf-lsCJeJBRcG

15. Cuncic, A. (2024, February 12). 7 Active Listening Techniques for Better Communication. *Verywell Mind.* https://www.verywellmind.com/what-is-active-listening-3024343

16. DIY Wall Art Sparks Joy And Creativity At Home - Crafting With Donna. (2023, May 28). *Crafting with Donna - Let's Enjoy Crafting Together.* https://craftingwithdonna.com/painting-and-drawing-ideas/diy-wall-art-sparks-joy-and-creativity-at-home/

17. Effective Communication: Improving Your Interpersonal Skills. (2018, November 3). *HelpGuide.org.* https://www.helpguide.org/relationships/communication/effective-communication

18.   Erin Wilkey. (2019, March 25). Teachers' Essential Guide to Cyberbullying Prevention. *Common Sense Education.* https://www.commonsense.org/education/articles/teachers-essential-guide-to-cyberbullying-prevention

19.   Fairfax County Public Schools. (2019). How to Handle Peer Pressure | Fairfax County Public Schools. *Fcps.edu.* https://www.fcps.edu/student-wellness-tips/peer-pressure

20.   FasterCapital. (n.d.). User generated content: DIY projects: DIY projects: Crafting creativity at home. Retrieved from https://www.fastercapital.com/content/User-generated-content--DIY-Projects--DIY-Projects--Crafting-Creativity-at-Home.html

21.   Federal Trade Commission. (2022). How To Recognize and Avoid Phishing Scams. *Consumer Information.* https://consumer.ftc.gov/articles/how-recognize-and-avoid-phishing-scams

22.   Godreau, J. (2024, April 19). Digital Detox: How To Reclaim Control of Your Screen Time and Boost Happiness. *Mindful Health Solutions.* https://mindfulhealthsolutions.com/digital-detox-how-to-reclaim-control-of-your-screen-time-and-boost-happiness/

23.   Google@EnvisionMarketingMA.com. (2017). How to clear your clogged drain with common household items. *Rodger's Plumbing.* Retrieved from https://www.rodgersplumbing.com/clear-clogged-drain-common-household-items/

24.   Heine, A. (2023, March 7). How to Dress for a Job Interview | Indeed.com. *Indeed.com.* https://www.indeed.com/career-advice/interviewing/how-to-dress-for-a-job-interview

25.   Herrity, J. (2017). 21 Job Interview Tips: How to Make a Great Impression | Indeed.com. *Indeed.com.* https://www.indeed.com/career-advice/interviewing/job-interview-tips-how-to-make-a-great-impression

26.   How interest works on a savings account. (n.d.). *Fortune Recommends.* https://fortune.com/recommends/banking/how-interest-works-on-savings-account/

27. How to Balance Academics and Social Life in College: Tips from a William Peace University Student | William Peace University. (2023, October 24). Www.peace.edu. https://www.peace.edu/how-to-balance-academics-and-social-life-in-college-tips-from-a-william-peace-university-student/

28. How to Handle Peer Pressure. (n.d.). Www.sedonasky.org. https://www.sedonasky.org/blog/how-to-handle-peer-pressure

29. How to make a Resume (with examples). (2023, February 28). *Indeed Career Guide*. https://www.indeed.com/career-advice/resumes-cover-letters/how-to-make-a-resume-with-examples

30. How to stop procrastinating: 9 tips for focus and productivity. (n.d.). *Calm Blog*. https://www.calm.com/blog/how-to-stop-procrastinating

31. Johnson, B. (2023, September 7). Teaching Kids Financial Responsibility with Card Controls | BankSouth Blog. *BankSouth*. https://banksouth.com/blog/teaching-kids-financial-responsibility-using-card-controls/

32. Joseph. (2024, March 20). 7 Steps to Diagnose and Fix Your Leaky Faucet. *Care and Repair*. https://careandrepair.com/blog/7-steps-to-fix-leaky-faucet/

33. Kim, S., Munten, S., Stafford, S., & Kolla, N. J. (2023, June 22). Can mindfulness play a role in building social-emotional capacities among youth exposed to screens? https://doi.org/10.3389/fpsyt.2023.1165217

34. Kopp, C. M. (2021, November 3). How Interest Rates Work on Savings Accounts. *Investopedia*. https://www.investopedia.com/articles/personal-finance/062315/how-interest-rates-work-savings-accounts.asp

35. Leaky Faucet Repair: DIY Fixes For Dripping Faucets - Western Rooter & Plumbing. (2023, October 5). *Western Rooter*. https://westernrooter.com/leaky-faucet-repair-diy-fixes-for-dripping-faucets/

36. Lerner, F. B. M. L. has 25+ years of experience as a freelance journalist S. was the winner of T. P. G. A. for B. F. C. L. about our editorial policies M. (n.d.). Keeping Your Debit Card Transactions Safe. *Investopedia*. https://www.investopedia.com/financial-edge/0312/how-to-keep-your-debit-card-transactions-safe.aspx

37. Mandal, E., & Lip, M. (2021). *Mindfulness, relationship quality, and conflict resolution strategies used by partners in close relationships.* Current Issues in Personality Psychology. https://doi.org/10.5114/cipp.2021.111981

38. Mayo Clinic. (2023). Support groups: Make connections, get help. *Mayo Clinic.* https://www.mayoclinic.org/healthy-lifestyle/stress-management/in-depth/support-groups/art-20044655

39. Mayo Clinic. (2023, August 10). Stress Management. *Mayo Clinic.* https://www.mayoclinic.org/healthy-lifestyle/stress-management/in-depth/stress-symptoms/art-20050987

40. Microsoft. (2021). Protect yourself from phishing. *Support.microsoft.com.* https://support.microsoft.com/en-us/windows/protect-yourself-from-phishing-0c7ea947-ba98-3bd9-7184-430e1f860a44

41. Mind Tools Content Team. (2023). MindTools | Home. Www.mindtools.com. https://www.mindtools.com/ak2ljl6/effective-scheduling

42. Overall, N. C., & McNulty, J. K. (2017, February). What type of communication during conflict is beneficial for intimate relationships? *Current Opinion in Psychology.* https://doi.org/10.1016/j.copsyc.2016.03.002

43. Prabhu, A. (2022, November 25). Importance of Scheduling Tasks and its Benefits. *Best OKR Software by Profit.co.* https://www.profit.co/blog/task-management/importance-of-scheduling-tasks-and-its-benefits/

44. Quizlet. (n.d.). Unit 1: Career exploration flashcards. Retrieved from https://quizlet.com/549493794/unit-1-career-exploration-flash-cards/

45. Resume & Cover Letter Guide | Community College of Philadelphia. (2024). *Myccp.online.* https://www.myccp.online/career-connections/resume-cover-letter-guide

46. SMART Goal Setting in Middle School, High School and Beyond | Open Door Education. (n.d.). *Open Door Education.* https://opendoor.education/smart-goal-setting-in-middle-school-high-school-and-beyond/

47. StopBullying.gov. (2019, September 24). Prevent Cyberbullying. *StopBullying.gov.* https://www.stopbullying.gov/cyberbullying/prevention

48. Support Groups: Types, Benefits, and What to Expect. (2021, July 21). *HelpGuide.org.* https://www.helpguide.org/mental-health/treatment/support-groups

49. Tennant, K., Butler, T. J. T., & Long, A. (2023, September 13). Active Listening. *Nih.gov; StatPearls Publishing.* https://www.ncbi.nlm.nih.gov/books/NBK442015/

50. thogan. (2023, June 27). The Most Common Causes of Drain Clogs and How to Prevent Them - Ray The Plumber. *Ray the Plumber.* https://raytheplumber.com/uncategorized/the-most-common-causes-of-drain-clogs-and-how-to-prevent-them/

51. True Value. (2020, November 24). Proper Tool Maintenance - True Value Hardware. *True Value Hardware.* https://www.truevalue.com/diy-projects/maintenance-and-repair/proper-tool-maintenance/

52. What Looks Good on College Applications? (n.d.). Www.princetonreview.com. https://www.princetonreview.com/college-advice/what-looks-good-on-college-applications

53. What are "Coping Skills" and How to Use Them. (2020, May 5). *Talkspace.* https://www.talkspace.com/blog/coping-skills-methods/

54. Wilson, C. (2023, August 17). Healthy Coping Mechanisms: 9 Adaptive Strategies to Try. *PositivePsychology.com.* https://positivepsychology.com/healthy-coping-mechanisms/

55. world, I. (2023, March 5). Beat Procrastination: The Power Of Accountability - Isa's world Life Coach - Medium. *Medium.* https://medium.com/@isasworldlc/beat-procrastination-the-power-of-accountability-b6cb99afe412

Bonus Chapter 1

Leadership and Empowerment

Leadership and Empowerment

Ever wondered what it takes to truly make a difference? Leadership and empowerment are more than just buzzwords—they're essential skills that every teen girl should embrace. Whether you're looking to boost your own confidence or inspire those around you, learning to cultivate leadership qualities is crucial. But don't think it's about fitting into a certain mold or changing who you are. Leadership is as unique and dynamic as your personality, and discovering your own style can be an exciting and empowering journey.

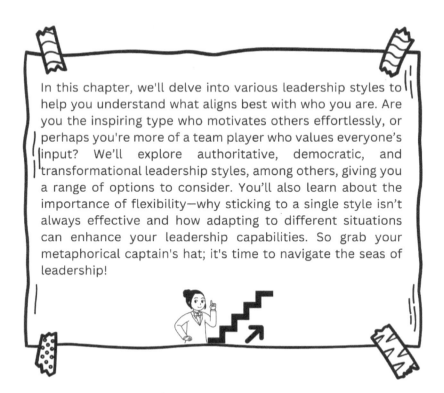

In this chapter, we'll delve into various leadership styles to help you understand what aligns best with who you are. Are you the inspiring type who motivates others effortlessly, or perhaps you're more of a team player who values everyone's input? We'll explore authoritative, democratic, and transformational leadership styles, among others, giving you a range of options to consider. You'll also learn about the importance of flexibility—why sticking to a single style isn't always effective and how adapting to different situations can enhance your leadership capabilities. So grab your metaphorical captain's hat; it's time to navigate the seas of leadership!

Exploring Different Leadership Styles

Let's dive into the world of leadership styles! As teen girls just stepping into leadership roles, understanding these different styles can empower you to find what works best for you and your unique personality.

First up, let's define some popular leadership styles. **Authoritative leaders** are often described as firm but fair. They set clear expectations and directions, making decisions with confidence. **Democratic leaders,** on the other hand, love to collaborate. They value feedback from their team members before making any big choices. This style is all about inclusivity and teamwork. **Transformational leaders** are all about inspiration. They have a vision and motivate others to strive for the same goals, creating an environment of continuous improvement and innovation.

Now, let's make one thing clear: there isn't a 'one-size-fits-all' when it comes to leadership styles. The key here is recognizing that effective leadership can come in many forms. For example, some situations might call for an authoritative approach where clear guidance is necessary. Other times, a democratic style might be more effective, especially if the goal is to foster creative solutions and team input.

Take a moment to think about your own experiences in team settings. Have you ever noticed how you naturally tend to take charge? Maybe you're the type who likes to gather everyone's ideas before making a decision, hinting at a democratic tendency. Or perhaps you're the motivator in the group who keeps everyone energized and focused on the end goal, which sounds like a transformational leader. Reflecting on these past experiences can give you insights into your natural inclinations and help you understand your leadership preferences better. Plus, a bit of self-reflection can be quite eye-opening!

But here's a cool thing about leadership - it's not static. You don't have to stick to one style forever. Flexibility is vital. Imagine being in a situation where a quick decision is needed; an authoritative approach might save the day. On another occasion, when fostering creativity is crucial, switching to a more democratic style could be beneficial. Being able to adapt your leadership style based on context is a powerful trait.

When thinking about flexibility, consider this guideline: next time you're part of a team project, try consciously switching up your leadership style to see what feels comfortable and what doesn't. Take note of how your team responds and which situations benefit most from each style. (Gomez, 2023)

To help you with this, jot down a list of scenarios where different styles might come in handy. For instance, during a group study session, you might adopt a democratic style to ensure everyone's ideas are heard. In a high-pressure game or competition, an authoritative style might keep everyone laser-focused. Trying out various styles will make you versatile and help you decide which resonates best with your innate strengths and the needs of the moment.

Also, it's important to remember that even though we've discussed specific styles, real-life leadership isn't always about sticking to one label. Many successful leaders blend elements from different styles depending on what's needed at the time. It's like having a toolkit – sometimes you need a hammer, other times a screwdriver.

Let's sprinkle in a bit of humor — because who says leadership can't be fun? Think of leadership styles like picking an outfit for the day. Sometimes you feel like rocking a power suit (authoritative), other days, a comfy tee and jeans (democratic). And occasionally, you go all out with glitter and glam to dazzle everyone (transformational). The right style depends on where you're going and what you need to achieve.

Ways to Take Initiative in School and Community

All right, let's talk leadership and empowerment! Whether you're at school, in your community, or even at home, you have countless opportunities to step up and make a difference. The goal here is to get you inspired and ready to take proactive steps in your environment, cultivating a sense of agency and responsibility. Let's jump into it!

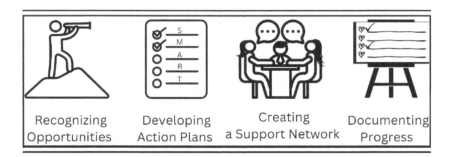

Recognizing Opportunities | Developing Action Plans | Creating a Support Network | Documenting Progress

Recognizing Opportunities

So, how do you spot leadership opportunities around you? Well, first things first: keep your eyes peeled! Opportunities can pop up where you least expect them. For example, if your school club needs someone to organize an event, that's an opportunity. If you notice something in your community that needs improvement, like a park that could use some cleaning, that's another chance to lead.

Next, listen actively. Often, people around you will indirectly mention problems or areas needing attention. Pay attention during class meetings, family dinners, or even casual hangouts with friends. Hearing statements like "I wish someone would..." or "Why doesn't anyone...?" can be your cue to step in.

Lastly, trust your gut. Sometimes, you just have a feeling that something needs doing, even if no one else has pointed it out. Go with that instinct. Leadership often begins with a simple idea that others haven't noticed yet.

Developing Action Plans

Alright, you've found your opportunity—now what? Creating actionable steps is key. Start by breaking down your big idea into smaller, manageable tasks. Think of it like a giant pizza; you can't eat it all at once but slice by slice, you can handle it.

Set clear goals. What do you want to achieve? Make these goals SMART—Specific, Measurable, Achievable, Relevant, and Time-bound. Say you want to start a recycling program at school. A specific goal might be: "I will get 50 students to sign up for the recycling program within the next two months."

Plan your actions step-by-step. List everything you need to do to meet your goal. Do you need to talk to teachers or administrators for approval? Do you need to gather materials? Do you need volunteers? Write all this down.

Delegate tasks. You don't have to do everything yourself. Assign different tasks to team members based on their strengths. Maybe one friend is great at designing posters, while another excels at speaking to groups.

Creating a Support Network

Leadership isn't a solo act; it's more like being the lead singer in a band. You need a support network to help you hit all the high notes. Building alliances starts with open communication. Talk to your peers about your ideas and listen to theirs as well. Be inclusive and inviting.

Identify potential allies. Who shares your interests and goals? Approach them and discuss how they can get involved. Be genuine and transparent about what you're trying to achieve and why you need their help.

Next, establish regular check-ins. Having weekly or bi-weekly meetings keeps everyone on the same page. Use these meetings to update each other on progress, address challenges, and brainstorm solutions. It also helps in building trust and camaraderie among the group.

Show appreciation. Simple gestures like saying "thank you" can go a long way in maintaining morale. Celebrate small victories as a team, whether it's through verbal praise, a shoutout on social media, or even a small celebratory treat.

Documenting Progress

Tracking accomplishments is crucial not just for your own growth but also for staying motivated. Keep a journal or a digital log of your activities and achievements. Note down what was effective and what wasn't, so you can learn from both successes and failures.

Create a visual progress tracker, like a chart or a bulletin board where you can mark off completed tasks and milestones. Seeing tangible evidence of your progress can be incredibly motivating for you and your team.

Reflect regularly. Set aside time to review what you've accomplished and what still needs attention. Ask yourself questions like: What worked well? What could we do differently next time? How did the team function together?

Share your progress with others. This could be through social media updates, newsletter articles, or presentations at school assemblies. When people see the impact of your leadership, they are more likely to support your future initiatives.

Mentoring and Supporting Peers

Mentorship is a rewarding experience that not only helps the mentee but also enriches the mentor's life. It's like having a wise and trusted friend who can guide you through life's challenges. Imagine being able to chat with someone who's been through it all before and can offer valuable advice, whether it's about school, personal issues, or future plans. The benefits are immense—mentors provide wisdom, encouragement, and a different perspective on issues you're facing (Hill et al., 2022). Plus, having a mentor can boost your confidence and help you feel supported.

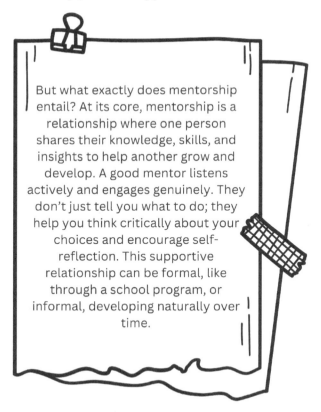

But what exactly does mentorship entail? At its core, mentorship is a relationship where one person shares their knowledge, skills, and insights to help another grow and develop. A good mentor listens actively and engages genuinely. They don't just tell you what to do; they help you think critically about your choices and encourage self-reflection. This supportive relationship can be formal, like through a school program, or informal, developing naturally over time.

Being an effective mentor involves more than just lending an ear. Here are some practical tips to consider. First, active listening is crucial. This means really paying attention to what your peer is saying without interrupting. Show empathy and try to understand their point of view. Second, genuine engagement is key. Ask open-ended questions that encourage deeper thinking, rather than yes or no answers. For example, instead of asking "Did you like the class?" you could ask "What did you learn from the class that you found interesting?"

Creating a safe and supportive environment for peers is another critical aspect of effective mentorship. One way to achieve this is by organizing peer-led workshops or discussion groups. Such gatherings can provide a platform for everyone to share their thoughts and experiences in a non-judgmental space. For instance, you could set up a weekly or monthly meeting where everyone gets a chance to speak about their challenges and successes. Make sure that these sessions are inclusive and respectful, encouraging everyone to participate.

Recognizing each other's successes and milestones is vital for motivation. Celebrating achievements, no matter how small, can have a huge positive impact on morale. Whether it's acing an exam, winning a sports match, or simply managing to speak up in class, acknowledging these victories helps build a supportive community. You could create a "Wall of Fame" where accomplishments are posted, or take a moment in your meetings to highlight individual successes.

Proactive steps can make these initiatives more impactful. For instance, to foster a culture of recognition, you might implement a buddy system where peers pair up to keep tabs on each other's progress and celebrate wins together. Alternatively, consider launching an awards ceremony at the end of each term to honor those who have made significant strides or contributed positively to the group.

As you build these mentorship and support networks, remember that flexibility and adaptability are important. Everyone has their unique strengths and challenges, so tailor your approach to fit individual needs. Be open to feedback and ready to adjust methods as needed. This willingness to evolve shows commitment and can help keep the group dynamic and responsive.

The value of mentorship and peer support as elements of leadership cannot be overstated. When young leaders support each other, they create a ripple effect of positivity and growth. Not only do they develop essential leadership qualities like communication, empathy, and problem-solving, but they also build lasting relationships that can serve as a foundation for future endeavors.

This supportive network plays a critical role in empowering teen girls to embrace their potential. It teaches them that leadership isn't a solitary journey but a collaborative effort. By fostering environments where everyone feels valued and heard, we cultivate communities that thrive on mutual respect and shared goals.

Empowering oneself and others through mentorship is a powerful way to make a difference in your community and school. It promotes personal growth and social responsibility, preparing you to face future challenges with resilience and confidence. So go ahead, step up, and take on the role of a mentor. Encourage your peers to do the same. You'll find that by lifting others, you also rise.

Building a Personal Leadership Style

Crafting a unique leadership style that reflects your personality and values can be both exciting and challenging. To start, let's dive into some activities that can help you reflect on your values, goals, and leadership influences.

Self-Reflection Exercises

Understanding your core values is crucial to developing a leadership style that's true to who you are. Grab a journal and take some time to think about what really matters to you. Here are some questions to get you started:

1. **What are my top three personal values?**
2. **Why are these values important to me?**
3. **Who are the leaders I admire and why?**

You could also create a vision board. Cut out pictures and words from magazines that resonate with your aspirations and values. This visual representation can serve as a constant reminder of the kind of leader you want to be.

Incorporating Personal Values

Once you've identified your values, it's time to integrate them into your leadership approach. Let's say one of your core values is honesty. You can demonstrate this by always being transparent with your team. If you're leading a school project, make it a point to openly share what needs to be done, including the challenges. This builds trust and sets a tone for open communication.

Another technique is value-based decision making. Before making a decision, ask yourself, "Does this align with my core values?" For instance, if fairness is important to you, ensure that everyone in your group has an equal opportunity to contribute.

Experimenting with Leadership Roles

Leadership isn't one-size-fits-all; it's more like trying on different outfits until you find the perfect fit. Don't be afraid to experiment with different leadership positions to see what suits you best. Whether it's leading a club, organizing a community event, or spearheading a class project, each experience will offer valuable lessons.

For example, if you've always been a behind-the-scenes person, try stepping up to a more visible role. It might feel uncomfortable at first, but you'll gain confidence and new skills along the way. Remember, every leadership role offers a chance to discover more about yourself and others.

Hands-On Experience

"Practice makes perfect" couldn't be truer when it comes to leadership. The more you lead, the more comfortable you'll become. Take every opportunity you can to put yourself in leadership positions. These experiences don't have to be grand; even small tasks like organizing a study group can offer meaningful insights.

Volunteering is another excellent way to gain hands-on experience. It not only helps you develop leadership skills but also allows you to give back to your community. Whether it's helping at a local shelter or coaching a junior sports team, these experiences can be incredibly fulfilling and enlightening.

Staying Authentic

One of the most important things to remember as you develop your leadership style is to stay authentic. People can tell when you're not being genuine, and it can erode trust and credibility. Embrace your quirks and unique traits—they're what set you apart.

For instance, if you have a knack for making people laugh, use humor to motivate your team and lighten the mood during stressful times. Or if you're naturally empathetic, show genuine concern for your team members' well-being. (Source: *Strategies for Developing Your Unique Leadership Style*, n.d.)

Embracing Uniqueness

Every leader is different, and that's a good thing! Celebrate what makes you unique instead of trying to conform to someone else's idea of a leader. Your individuality is your strength. Let's say you're introverted and prefer smaller group settings—use this to your advantage by building strong, one-on-one relationships with your team members.

Encourage others to embrace their uniqueness too. Diversity brings a wealth of perspectives and ideas that can lead to innovative solutions and a more inclusive environment. By valuing authenticity and uniqueness, you create a culture where everyone feels empowered to bring their whole selves to the table.

Seeking Feedback

Another essential aspect of developing your leadership style is seeking feedback. Encourage honest and constructive feedback from your peers and mentors. Ask questions like, "What do you think I did well?" and "How can I improve?"

Reflect on the feedback and use it to make adjustments. Maybe you'll find out that you need to work on better delegating tasks, or perhaps you'll learn that your communication style needs refining. Whatever the feedback, take it in stride and use it as a tool for growth.

Creating a Culture of Continuous Improvement

By actively seeking and acting on feedback, you also set an example for your team. When they see you committed to growing and improving, they'll be inspired to do the same. This creates a culture of continuous improvement, where everyone feels encouraged to develop and refine their skills.

Imagine you're leading a group project and you receive feedback that the team meetings are too long and unfocused. Acknowledge the feedback and make changes, like setting clear agendas and time limits for meetings. This not only improves efficiency but also shows your team that you value their input and are willing to make changes for the collective good.

Practicing Self-Awareness and Emotional Intelligence

Effective leadership requires self-awareness and emotional intelligence. Self-awareness allows you to understand your emotions, strengths, and areas for development. Emotional intelligence helps you manage your emotions and understand the emotions of others.

Take time to reflect on your emotional responses in different situations. How do you react under pressure? What triggers stress for you? Understanding these aspects of yourself can help you navigate challenging situations more effectively.

Work on developing empathy by actively listening to your team members. Show genuine interest in their concerns and feelings. This helps build strong, trusting relationships and fosters a positive work environment.

Developing a leadership style that works for you is a journey, not a destination. It involves continuous self-reflection, learning, and adapting. By understanding your personality, identifying your leadership values, gaining hands-on experience, and embracing your uniqueness, you can craft a leadership style that is both authentic and effective.

ALEX AND RILEY HARPER

Wow, we've covered a lot about leadership styles! By now, you should have a good idea of what kind of leader you might want to be. Remember, whether you're channeling your inner authoritative boss lady, being the democratic team player, or inspiring everyone around you as a transformational leader, there's no wrong way to lead. Mix and match these styles like your favorite outfits until you find the combo that fits you just right. And hey, don't stress if your style evolves over time—that's all part of the fun!

So, next time you're stepping up in school or community projects, think about how you can adapt your leadership based on the situation. Try out different styles, see what works, and learn from each experience. Leadership is all about growing and learning, not just for yourself but also for those you lead. Keep it flexible, keep it fun, and most importantly, keep being awesome!

Bonus Chapter 2

Self-Defense and Personal Safety

Self-Defense and Personal Safety

Want to feel more confident in your everyday life? Self-defense and personal safety aren't about becoming a superhero overnight—they're about learning a few practical tips and tricks to stay safe. Whether you're walking home from school, traveling alone, or hanging out with friends, these skills can empower you to handle unexpected situations. Plus, you'll get to channel your inner ninja without ever needing a black belt!

In this chapter, we'll explore everything from basic self-defense techniques that target vulnerable spots on an attacker to breaking free from holds like wrist grabs and bear hugs. You'll also learn how to use everyday items like keys and pens as improvised weapons and discover the power of your voice for scaring off threats.

We'll discuss the importance of carrying self-defense tools such as pepper spray and personal alarms, and touch on situational awareness so you can avoid danger before it happens. Plus, we'll cover how to practice these moves regularly so they become second nature. Let's get started on making you feel safer and more prepared in any situation!

Basic Self-Defense Techniques

Alright girls, let's dive into some self-defense techniques that can help you feel more confident and ready to handle any sticky situation. Remember, self-defense isn't about being able to do backflips or becoming a martial arts master—it's about knowing a few simple moves and skills that can make all the difference.

First up, let's talk about striking vulnerable areas. Imagine if someone tries to attack you; your best bet is to go for the spots that hurt the most. The eyes, nose, and groin are prime targets. Aim a jab at the eyes to temporarily blind your attacker, giving you a chance to escape. A swift punch to the nose can cause extreme pain and disorientation—trust me, they won't know what hit them! And don't forget about the groin; a well-placed kick or knee strike there can incapacitate an attacker pretty quickly (H, 2023).

Next, let's practice breaking free from common holds or grabs. You might find yourself in a situation where someone grabs your wrist or puts you in a bear hug. In these cases, it's crucial to know how to wriggle out. For example, if someone grabs your wrist, twist your hand towards the thumb and pull away—this works because the grip is weakest there. Another technique is using your elbows in a bear hug scenario; aim a sharp elbow strike to the ribs or stomach. These quick moves make it easier for you to break free and run for safety.

Now, let's get creative with improvised weapons. You've got more tools at your disposal than you realize! Everyday objects like keys, pens, or even your phone can be turned into self-defense weapons. Hold your key between your fingers when walking alone, ready to use it as a makeshift knuckle duster if needed. Pens can serve as excellent stabbing tools against an attacker's hands or face. Even a tightly rolled magazine can act as a baton if you're in a pinch. The idea here is to use anything at hand to create a barrier between you and your attacker (Instructables, 2015).

One of the most underrated but powerful tools you have is your voice. Not only can yelling attract attention, but it can also scare off potential attackers. Shouting "fire" instead of "help" often gets more immediate reactions from bystanders. Your voice can catch people's attention and might startle the attacker enough to give you precious moments to get away. Practice shouting confidently and assertively; it might feel silly, but it's better to be prepared!

You might think carrying self-defense tools like pepper spray or personal alarms sounds a bit over-the-top, but these gadgets can really be lifesavers. Pepper spray is relatively easy to find and straightforward to use. Just aim for the face and spray to cause temporary blindness and pain, giving you time to flee. Personal alarms are small devices that emit a loud noise when activated, drawing people's attention to your situation (H, 2023).

Let's take a breather here and recap a bit. We've covered attacking vulnerable spots, breaking free from holds, using everyday items as weapons, and the power of your voice. Knowing these basics can significantly enhance your ability to protect yourself.

Let's say you're walking home from school and a stranger starts following you. You've got your keys ready in your hand (pointy end out), and you're staying alert. Your heart's pounding, but you remember everything we've talked about. If things escalate, you know precisely where to strike and how to use your voice. This preparedness can make all the difference.

Okay, now let's slow down a bit and think about practicing these techniques regularly. It's not enough to just read about them; you need to be comfortable performing these actions. You could practice with friends or family members in a safe environment. Regularly practicing these moves will make you more confident and quicker to react in real-life situations.

And don't just stop at self-defense moves; consider joining a self-defense class. Many classes are specifically designed for teenage girls and teach practical skills in a safe, supportive environment. Plus, you'll probably make friends who share your interest in staying safe.

Lastly, let's touch on situational awareness—the ability to notice what's happening around you. Stay alert, keep your head up, and be mindful of your surroundings. Avoid distractions like your phone when you're walking alone, and always trust your instincts. If something doesn't feel right, it probably isn't.

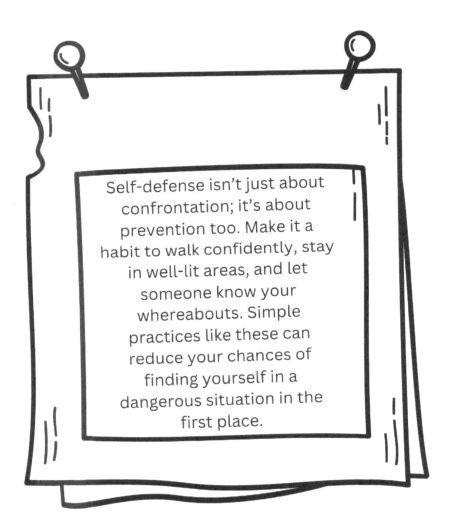

Self-defense isn't just about confrontation; it's about prevention too. Make it a habit to walk confidently, stay in well-lit areas, and let someone know your whereabouts. Simple practices like these can reduce your chances of finding yourself in a dangerous situation in the first place.

Staying Aware

Staying alert and avoiding danger is all about developing smart habits and staying aware of your surroundings. These skills can make a huge difference in ensuring your safety. Let's dive into some essential tips that can help you become more vigilant and proactive.

First off, it's crucial to develop the habit of regularly scanning your environment. This means every time you enter a new space or even while walking in familiar areas, take a moment to observe what's going on around you. Notice any unusual activity, like a person who seems out of place or is acting suspiciously. For example, if you're at a coffee shop and someone keeps glancing around nervously or hovering near personal belongings that aren't theirs, it's worth being cautious. By becoming more observant, you can spot potential dangers before they escalate.

Next, let's talk about personal distractions, especially those pesky smartphones. We all love our phones, but they can be a real distraction when we're out and about. When you're walking alone, do yourself a favor and put the phone away. Texts, calls, and social media updates can wait. Keeping your eyes and ears open allows you to react quickly if something feels off. For instance, you might notice a car driving slowly alongside you or hear footsteps behind you. Staying alert gives you that extra edge to stay safe and make better decisions.

One of the most powerful tools you have is your intuition. Trust your instincts. If something feels wrong, it probably is. Don't worry about seeming paranoid or overreacting. Your gut feelings are there for a reason. If you find yourself in a situation that makes you uneasy—whether it's a deserted parking lot or someone invading your personal space—remove yourself from it. It's always better to be safe than sorry.

High-risk locations and scenarios are exactly where we don't want to find ourselves, especially alone. Places like isolated areas, poorly lit streets, or taking nighttime walks may seem harmless during the day but can turn risky after dark. Avoid these spots whenever possible. If you need to go somewhere that's not safe, try to bring a friend along. Having company significantly reduces the chances of becoming a target.

Walking with a buddy is one of the simplest yet most effective ways to stay safe. Whether you're heading home from a party or just making a quick trip to the store, having someone with you deters potential threats. Plus, it's a great opportunity for some face-to-face social time, which is always a plus!

When you're flying solo at night, stick to well-lit areas and avoid shortcuts through alleys or secluded pathways. Streetlights and busy roads provide an extra layer of security, making it harder for someone to approach unnoticed. If you feel uneasy about where you parked your car, trust that feeling. Look for a spot closer to your destination, preferably in a well-lit area with lots of people around. Sometimes, calling a friend to walk you to your car isn't just okay—it's smart and responsible.

Being observant doesn't just mean looking around; it also involves listening. Keep an ear out for sounds like approaching footsteps, rustling bushes, or unfamiliar noises. These auditory cues can alert you to potential dangers before you see them. Similarly, your hands should be free so that you're ready to defend yourself or make a quick escape if needed. For example, have your car keys in hand before you leave a building, so you're not fumbling for them in a dark parking lot.

Another tip is to make intelligent use of technology. Apps like personal safety alerts and location sharing can be lifesavers. Share your travel routes and estimated arrival times with trusted friends or family members. This way, someone always knows where you are and can act if something goes wrong.

In addition to these tips, remember that group activities are generally safer than being alone. Join clubs or groups that encourage companionship, whether it's a morning jogging club, a night class, or simply coordinating schedules with a roommate or friend for activities.

Teenage girls, in particular, should be cautious about oversharing on social media. Broadcasting your location in real-time can make you an easy target. Save those check-ins and status updates for later when you're back home safely. Adjust privacy settings to limit who can see your posts, and be selective about accepting friend requests from people you don't know well.

Lastly, don't underestimate the power of setting up emergency contacts on your phone. Have a few reliable people saved as favorites so you can reach them quickly if anything happens. It's also useful to learn basic self-defense moves. Even simple techniques, like knowing how to break free from a wrist grab, can make a significant difference in an emergency.

Safety on the Go

When it comes to staying safe during travel, planning is the key. First and foremost, plan your route ahead of time and share it with someone you trust. This might sound like a hassle, but having a clear idea of where you're going ensures you won't end up lost in an unfamiliar place. Ever tried to navigate through a maze without a map? Yeah, that's what not planning your route feels like. So whip out those maps or apps, get your route down pat, and make sure a friend or family member knows your game plan.

Next up, stay in well-lit, populated areas, especially when walking alone. Think of it this way: darkness and isolation are like the dynamic duo of danger. If you're wandering through dimly lit alleys, it's easier for potential threats to hide in the shadows. Bright lights and crowds provide safety in numbers and visibility. So channel your inner moth and stick to the brightest places you can find!

Now let's talk about situational awareness when using public transportation. Public transport can be a wild ride – quite literally sometimes. Be aware of your surroundings and people around you. Imagine you're a detective, always keeping an eye out for anything unusual. Notice who gets on and off, if anyone's acting sketchy, or if someone's been following you like they're auditioning for a spy movie. Trust your gut; if something feels off, it probably is.

And here's a handy trick: use travel apps or tools that enhance your safety, like GPS tracking or ride-sharing services. Ever felt like you needed superpowers to keep tabs on your whereabouts? Well, there's an app for that! Most smartphones have built-in GPS tracking, which you can share with trusted contacts. Ride-sharing services usually come with features to help ensure you're safely on your way, like confirming the driver and car details before you hop in. No more jumping into random cars and hoping for the best. Use these digital helpers to stay safe on the go.

Beyond merely planning, consider the specifics. Knowing the safe spots along your route matters. Are there friendly cafes, police stations, or shops you can duck into if needed? Familiarizing yourself with these locations ensures you've got backup options in case things turn south. Having alternatives lined up is like having extra lives in a video game – you hope not to use them, but they're there just in case.

Moreover, don't forget to have the right gear with you. Carry essential items like your phone, ID, some cash, and perhaps even a personal alarm. These aren't just items; they are components of your safety toolkit. A charged phone keeps you connected, an ID helps authorities identify you in case of emergencies, and a bit of cash can be a lifesaver if electronic payments fail for some reason. Oh, and a personal alarm? It's like having an emergency siren ready to go, which can scare away potential threats and attract help from others around.

Let's dive a bit deeper into using public transport safely. For example, if you're on a bus or a train, try to sit near the driver or in a busy compartment rather than an empty one at the back. The presence of more people and staff can deter potential mischief-makers. Also, it's smart to know the schedule and frequency of the public transport system you're using. Waiting alone at a deserted bus stop late at night isn't exactly the epitome of safety.

While we're on the topic, let's not ignore ride-shares and taxis. Always confirm that the vehicle you're getting into matches the details provided in the app. Check the license plate, car model, and the driver's photo. It sounds tedious but better safe than sorry. If your gut tells you something's off, don't hesitate to cancel the ride and report it to the service. Plus, most ride-share apps offer options to share your trip with others, which adds an extra layer of security – kind of like having a virtual buddy keeping an eye on you.

Speaking of safety-oriented apps, there are several worth mentioning. One such app is "bSafe", which comes loaded with features like voice-activated SOS alerts, live streaming to contacts, and location sharing. Another useful app is "Life360", designed specifically for families and close friends to keep track of each other's whereabouts. You can get real-time updates and check-in notifications, ensuring everyone stays in the loop. These aren't just apps; they're like having a digital guardian angel.

Don't overlook the basics either. Dress appropriately for the situation. If you're traveling in a conservative area, dressing modestly can help you avoid unwanted attention. Comfortable shoes are a must as well, especially if you'll be doing a lot of walking. They allow you to move quickly and safely - because there's nothing worse than trying to escape a dicey situation while hobbling on high heels.

Emergency Preparedness

When it comes to personal safety, creating a solid emergency plan is key. Imagine this: you're out with friends, having a blast, and suddenly something goes wrong. What do you do? Panic isn't the answer. Having a personal safety plan ensures you're prepared for whatever life throws your way. Let's dive into the essentials.

First, identify safe places and reliable contacts. Know where you can go if you're in trouble – like a nearby café or a well-lit public area. Memorize these spots so you don't have to think twice if an emergency arises. Also, make a list of trusted people you can call. Keep their numbers on speed dial. This could be family members, close friends, or even neighbors you're comfortable reaching out to in a pinch. Remember, quick access to help can make all the difference.

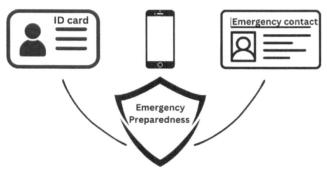

Next, carry essential items at all times. Your ID, phone, and a small card with emergency contacts are non-negotiables. Think of your phone as your lifeline – it's not just for selfies and browsing social media. Make sure it's always charged before heading out. An emergency contact card is useful if your phone dies or gets lost. Slip it into your wallet or bag. This way, anyone who finds you can reach out to someone you trust.

Now, let's talk about first aid skills. You don't need to be a medical expert, but knowing basic first aid can be incredibly helpful. Learn how to treat minor cuts, burns, or sprains. Simple things like cleaning a wound and applying a bandage can prevent infections and complications. There are plenty of online resources and local courses that teach these basics. Spending a few hours learning first aid could save you or someone else in an emergency situation.

Understanding different types of emergencies is crucial too. Whether it's natural disasters like earthquakes or dealing with active threats, your response should vary. For natural disasters, know the safest spots in buildings, like under sturdy furniture during an earthquake. In case of a fire, remember to stop, drop, and roll if your clothes catch fire. Active threats are scarier to think about, but it's vital to know what to do. Running away from the threat is usually the best first choice. If you can't run, hiding out of sight (preferably behind something solid) is the next best option. As a last resort, be prepared to defend yourself if you're directly confronted.

While crafting your emergency plan, consider scenarios specific to your lifestyle and location. Live in a flood-prone area? Have a waterproof bag ready with essentials. Regularly commute by train? Identify exits and familiarize yourself with evacuation protocols. The more tailored your plan, the more effective it will be.

Remember to discuss your safety plan with those you trust. Share your designated safe places and contacts with them. Having everyone on the same page ensures they can assist you better if needed. Practicing your plan occasionally isn't a bad idea either. It can make your reactions more instinctual rather than panicked.

Incorporate technology into your safety arsenal. There are multiple apps designed to enhance personal safety. Some apps send your location to selected contacts when you're in distress. Others provide real-time updates on local emergencies. Familiarize yourself with these tools and integrate them into your routine. They're modern solutions that can complement traditional safety practices.

One often overlooked aspect of personal safety planning is communication. Establish a check-in routine with someone you trust, especially if you're going somewhere unfamiliar or risky. A simple text saying, "Hey, I'm here," can keep someone aware of your whereabouts. If plans change, update them. It only takes a few seconds but can be incredibly reassuring for both parties.

It's also important to stay aware of your surroundings. Keep your head up, eyes scanning your environment. Avoid distractions like texting or listening to music at high volumes when walking alone. This slight shift in attention can significantly enhance your ability to notice potential threats early.

Lastly, mental preparation is part of your safety plan. Staying calm under pressure helps you make rational decisions. Practice deep breathing or grounding techniques to manage stress. Visualizing different scenarios and your responses to them can mentally prepare you for real-life situations.

Alright, girls, we've covered a ton of ground in this chapter! From learning how to strike those oh-so-vulnerable spots on an attacker to turning everyday items into makeshift weapons, you're now loaded with some solid self-defense knowledge. Remember, it's not about becoming the next action movie star but knowing these basic moves and being aware of your surroundings can make a huge difference. Whether you're practicing breaking free from holds or using your voice as a powerful tool, these techniques are all about keeping you safe and confident.

But self-defense isn't just about throwing punches; it's also about staying sharp and prepared. Keeping your phone handy, sharing your travel routes, and always staying alert to your environment can prevent many sketchy situations before they even start. Regularly practice these skills and consider taking a self-defense class—because, hey, why not turn safety into a social event? And don't forget, walking with a buddy and avoiding dark, isolated areas are simple yet effective habits. So, keep your head up, stay aware, and remember: your safety is in your hands!

BONUS CHAPTER
REFERENCES

1. 30 Tips for Women Living Alone | Stay Safe and Secure. (2024). *Reolink.com*. https://reolink.com/blog/safety-tips-for-single-women-living-alone/?srsltid=AfmBOoqT2uxbURQYj-1Qkl7902KLKHnEKaMXLCj4U8bKLJZ4HNd-OTFE

2. Becker, B. (2023, September 14). The 7 Most Common Leadership Styles & How to Find Your Own. *Hubspot.* https://blog.hubspot.com/marketing/leadership-styles

3. Coachingly. (2024). *Coachingly.ai.* https://www.coachingly.ai/blog/single/the-power-of-authentic-leadership-developing-your-unique-leadership-style

4. Essential Self Defense Tips That Every Woman Should Know. (2023, June 25). *Giveaways 4 Mom.* https://giveaways4mom.com/self-defense-for-women-tips/

5. Exploring Leadership Styles: Which One Resonates With You? (2023, October 3). Www.ollusa.edu. https://www.ollusa.edu/blog/leadership-styles.html

6. Grossman, D. (2024, April 8). Trust in the Workplace: 6 Steps to Building Trust with Employees. *Yourthoughtpartner.com.* https://www.yourthoughtpartner.com/blog/bid/59619/leaders-follow-these-6-steps-to-build-trust-with-employees-improve-how-you-re-perceived

7. Hill, S. E. M., Ward, W. L., Seay, A., & Buzenski, J. (2022, June 27). The Nature and Evolution of the Mentoring Relationship in Academic Health Centers. *Journal of Clinical Psychology in Medical Settings*. https://doi.org/10.1007/s10880-022-09893-6

8. How to Protect Yourself as a Woman: Safety Tips and Tools. (2024, August 5). *ResQ*. https://resqjewelry.com/blogs/news/how-to-protect-yourself-woman

9. Instructables. (2015, August 30). Basic Street Safety for Women. *Instructables*. https://www.instructables.com/Basic-Street-Safety-for-Women/

10. Lui, D. (2024, August 5). How to Protect Yourself as a Woman: Safety Tips and Tools. *ResQ*. https://resqjewelry.com/blogs/news/how-to-protect-yourself-woman

11. Personal Preparedness Planning. (n.d.). *United States Department of State*. https://www.state.gov/global-community-liaison-office/crisis-management/personal-preparedness-planning/

12. Planning for Safety | NHTSA. (n.d.). Www.nhtsa.gov. https://www.nhtsa.gov/planning-safer-school-bus-stops-and-routes/planning-safety

13. Purbasari, A. (2022, April 22). Leadership Mentoring: Benefits & Best Practices. *Chronus*. https://chronus.com/blog/best-practices-creating-leadership-mentoring-programs

14. Road Safety: Global Safety and Security - Northwestern University. (n.d.). Www.northwestern.edu. https://www.northwestern.edu/global-safety-security/health-safety/travel-safety/road-safety.html

15. Steinmann, B., Klug, H. J. P., & Maier, G. W. (2019, November 29). The Path Is the Goal: How Transformational Leaders Enhance Followers' Job Attitudes and Proactive Behavior. *Frontiers in Psychology; NCBI*. https://doi.org/10.3389/fpsyg.2018.02338

16. Strategies for Developing your Unique Leadership Style. (n.d.). Www.business-Pathways.com. https://www.business-pathways.com/blog/posts/strategies-develop-personal-leadership-style